MARQUE SPOTLIGHT SERIES NUMBER TWO

FORD ESCORT DOWNUNDER

Original text written and researched
by Cliff Chambers.

THE MARQUE SPOTLIGHT SERIES with ROADTESTS FROM MODERN MOTOR
is a unique series with a strong Australian accent. It highlights interesting individual car
models (and model series) by providing information, specifications, photographs and
contemporary material, including roadtests. It is aimed at owners, potential owners and
enthusiasts alike.

MARQUE
PUBLISHING COMPANY

Distributed by Universal Press
and
Gregory's Scientific Publications

MARQUE SPOTLIGHT SERIES NUMBER TWO
FORD ESCORT DOWNUNDER

Original text written and researched by Cliff Chambers.
Copyright 1989: Marque Publishing Company Pty Ltd.

First published in 1990 by Marque Publishing Company Pty Ltd
911 King Georges Road Blakehurst 2221 (PO Box 203, Hurstville 2220). Phone (02) 546 5521.

Ford Escort Downunder
ISBN: 0 947079 09 2

Proudly produced wholly within Australia.
Design and production by Tony Davis.
Copy editing by Anne Sahlin.
Cover by Irene Meier.
Typesetting and assembly by Type Forty, Glebe.
Photo screening, separations and printing by Globe Press Pty Ltd
50 Weston St, Brunswick Victoria 3056.

Photo sources: Automotive News Service, Marque Publishing Company, Ford Australia, Ford (UK) and Modern Motor magazine.

Marque Publishing Company would like to thank the following for their assistance, advice and sympathy: Barry Lake, Ken Croft, Cliff Chambers, Adrian Ryan and the PR staff at Ford, the crew at Universal Press and Gregory's and the publishers of Australia's leading monthly automotive magazine, Modern Motor, who have kindly allowed Marque to reproduce historic roadtests.

DISTRIBUTION BY:

UNIVERSAL PRESS:
64 Talavera Road, North Ryde NSW 2113. Phone (02) 888 1877. Fax (02) 888 9850.
GREGORY'S SCIENTIFIC PUBLICATIONS:
Sydney: 904 Bourke St, Waterloo 2015. Phone: (02) 698 1588. Fax (02) 698 3705.
Melbourne: 316 St Kilda Road, St Kilda 3182. Phone: (03) 534 0684. Fax (03) 537 1506.
Brisbane: 1 Manning St, Sth Brisbane 4101. Phone: (07) 844 1051. Fax (07) 844 4637.
Adelaide: 21 Wright St, Adelaide 5000. Phone: (08) 231 9944. Fax (08) 231 4046.
Perth: 'Herdsman Business Park' 38A Walters Drive, Osborne Park 6017. Ph: (09) 244 2488. Fax (09) 244 2554.
New Zealand: 33 Karaka St, Newton Auckland. Phone: 399 821. Fax 399 834.
Singapore: 39B Jalan Pemimpin # 03–02 Teck Long Building 2057. Phone: 259 2080. Fax 259 0600.

SPECIAL NOTE ON POWER OUTPUT AND SPECIFICATIONS:

Variance may be found in quoted specifications, particularly in power output figures, due to the different methods used for measuring engine power.

Except where otherwise stated, the mechanical specifications given for individual model cars are those issued by the manufacturer at the time each vehicle was released.

Unfortunately, different systems of measuring power have been used in Australia at various times. Each system can produce a different figure for the same engine.

In the early days of motoring, the most commonly used unit was the horsepower. The lack of an agreed method for measuring horsepower, however, led to the widespread use of an artificial system. This was instituted by the British Royal Automobile Club and was derived from a formula which included the bore diameter and the number of cylinders. It was expressed in rated horsepower (HP). As engine technology improved this rating became less accurate, giving figures well below the actual power output, but the system was still widely used, particularly by governments for taxation purposes. Even in the 1970s and early 1980s, some car companies announced rated HP figures for their engines. Where possible we have included these figures.

To gain a more valid guide to engine power, the system of measuring 'brake horsepower' on an engine dynamometer came into fashion. From the 1940s the US system of measuring 'SAE brake horsepower' was widely used. These figures (derived from test procedures developed by the Society of Automotive Engineers) provided the gross power of an engine without the exhaust system and some ancillary equipment fitted. The resulting figures were flattering (and became even more so as the companies found more and more ways to fudge the numbers), so in the 1970s there was a trend towards issuing net horsepower figures, measured with most or all of the engine equipment attached.

Different methods still produced different 'net' results but since 1976, when Australia adopted the SI metric system, the situation has improved. From 1976 all figures were measured in kilowatts, with 75 kW being approximately equal to 100 bhp, and the industry changed to 'installed power', which is based on an Australian standard similar to the German DIN system.

The result is power figures which are less flattering but much more accurate and comparable. In 1969, for example, Holden claimed 300 bhp for its top–line 1969 Monaro but in 1988 the company claimed only 180 kW (240 bhp) for its much more powerful fuel–injected 'Group A' V8. Ford Australia's figures took a similar tumble.

For the Marque Spotlight Series we have converted all figures (except rated horsepower) to kilowatts and, as a general rule, you can assume that figures are 'gross' up to the mid–1970s, then 'net' until the late 1970s/early 1980s when 'installed' figures became almost universal.

Performance figures too are subject to variation but we have endeavoured to check against as many sources as possible and give what we believe to be an accurate guide to the performance of each car when new.

Above: Bob Inglis in his Twin – Cam rally car.

Previous page: The 1979 Repco Reliability Trial was a thinly disguised race around Australia. John Bryson and Sonja Kable Cumming, teamed in this 2 – litre turbocharged Escort, finished 92nd (last) behind a Holden FJ. In their defence, they weren't giving their all, as demonstrated by the fact that they stopped to get married along the way. The major Ford effort concentrated on a team of Cortina sixes led by Colin Bond, but in the end the Holden Commodore proved victorious.

Title page: Rally ace Colin Bond in a Mark 2 at Sydney Showground.

COVER PHOTOS
Top left: An Aussie Escort Super.
Top Right: Escort Mark 2, fitted with the Escapee dress – up pack.
Bottom left: Racing driver Bob Holden lifts the inside wheel of a Twin – Cam.
Bottom Right: Colin Bond leading one of Ford's many unsuccessful attempts to put the Escort on the winner's podium in the Southern Cross International Rally.

Below: One of the 25 UK RS2000s specially imported by Ford Australia.

FORD ESCORT DOWNUNDER

TWO DECADES OF ESCORT

For more than 20 years, Ford's Escort has been among the world's most successful small cars. Initially built for the British market, the Escort quickly migrated to Europe, Australia and finally the United States. Now well into its third generation, the Escort has survived and prospered for many reasons, but mostly because of its versatility.

Like most of the world's biggest selling cars, the Escort was built to a formula which permitted a multitude of variations at minimal expense. At various times during its lifespan, the Escort has been sold in two – door and four – door sedan form, as a station wagon, panel van and even a cabriolet. A vast array of options allowed buyers to personalise even the most basic of cars.

In 1968, when the Escort made its British debut, it faced a market dominated by the products of a successful but single – minded BMC. Having reaped the benefits of Alec Issigonis' oustanding Mini design, BMC threw its entire philosophy behind the front – wheel drive concept. In contrast, the Escort emerged as a conventional – looking, rear – wheel drive 'three – box' sedan which was less space efficient than its BMC competitors and certainly less avant – garde.

But what the Escort offered in abundance was simplicity, variety and prices which were honed to attack every model in BMC's Mini/1100 line – up. To millions of conservative British car buyers, the Escort was manna from heaven.

The combination of a simple front engine/rear drive formula had served Ford faithfully since it began production of British models in the early 1930s. Designs like the Prefect and Anglia certainly weren't perfection on wheels but they endowed Ford with a reputation for cheap, easy servicing and durability. It was this philosophy which the Escort repackaged so successfully. Apart from its appeal to conservative British buyers, the Escort was also the ideal basis for a successful competition car. Strong, compact and easily modified, it was destined for greatness in a variety of motor sport events

ESCORTS DOWNUNDER

Prior to the Escort's arrival, Ford had never enjoyed success in the Australian small car market. During the 1950s and 1960s, a succession of Prefect and Anglia models was overshadowed by the rugged and inexpensive Morris Minor and Volkswagen. Not to mention the impact of the Morris Mini, which came in 1961.

But as the 1970s approached, Japan was becoming the dominant influence on Australian small car buyers, offering value and simplicity which existing European designs were hard – pressed to match. As the products of British Leyland, Fiat and even Volkswagen fell by the wayside, the Escort maintained Ford's presence in the Australian small car market by offering a variety of models backed by ingenious and far – sighted marketing.

Between 1970 and 1981, 146,849 Ford Escorts were sold in Australia. Produced in Mark 1 and Mark 2 form, locally assembled Escorts were available as two – door and four – door sedans with a wide variety of trim and engine options. To attract commercial buyers and the fabled 'recreational' user, an Escort panel van was produced. Regrettably, Australia missed out on the attractive Escort Estate (station wagon) model, but Ford kept the performance enthusiasts happy with occasional batches of fully imported RS models.

In addition to its mainstream line – up, the Escort's ten years of local production was punctuated by a string of special low – volume versions. Models like the 'Denim Pack', 'Escapee' and 'Sundowner' van meant that Ford Australia could position an Escort to exploit the tiniest of market 'niches' with volumes as low as 100 cars.

Today, long after the last Escort rolled down the production line of Ford's Sydney factory, the model's popularity remains unquestioned. A combination of sporting prowess, distinctive style and the robust performance of 2 – litre models has ensured growing popularity with drivers who appreciate the responsiveness and innate toughness of these endearing cars.

THE ESCORT ARRIVES

A thoroughly modern replacement for the aging and oddly styled 105E Anglia, Ford's Escort made its international debut in January 1968: right in the midst of the Northern Hemisphere winter. In Britain, it was traditional for new models to be released at the annual Earl's Court Motor Show. But since the Escort missed out on this venue, motoring journalists gained their first experience of the new car not on Britain's icy roads but in the sunny environment of Morocco in Northern Africa. The initial reaction to the new car was extremely favourable. Comments such as 'precise handling', 'modern looks' and 'super value' peppered the early British press reports.

In Britain, the Escort range began with the 1.1 – litre 'De Luxe' – a misnomer if ever there was one. This most basic of Escorts developed just 38 kW, had thinly padded seats, rubber floor mats and very little of anything else. Even in the depths of a British winter, the heater was optional. However, since it sold primarily to fleet buyers and its price was only marginally above that of a comparably equipped Mini, the De Luxe fulfilled an important role in the marketing strategy. For family buyers and those prepared to outlay a little more cash for improved comfort, there was the two – door 'Super' model. Still with the underpowered but frugal 1.1 – litre engine as standard and the 1.3 – litre an option, the Super included interior carpets, a cigar lighter and that all – important heater as standard.

With the Twin – Cam built in limited numbers and designed mainly for competition work, the pick of Ford's Escort Mark 1 range was the 1300GT. With the addition of a Weber carburettor, specially designed extractor exhaust system and other modifications, the GT delivered 56 kW and had a top speed in excess of 150 km/h. Improved seats, comprehensive instrumentation, carpets and woodgrain trim on the dashboard and door cappings added prestige without pushing the GT too far beyond the reach of average car buyers.

Taking the combination of roller – skate handling and brisk performance a giant step forward, the Escort Twin – Cam simply rewrote British motor sporting record books. With Australian – born Frank Gardner at the wheel, a Twin – Cam won the British Saloon Car title at its first attempt. In so doing, it not only disposed of contenders for class honours, but also outright division cars including Mustangs, Camaros and aging Jaguars.

On the rally circuit, Escorts (in both the 'under 1300 cc' and 'under 1600 cc' classes) won six international events and gained Ford the 1968 Rally Constructors Championship. In 1969, Ford again dominated the rally scene, with four victories and its second Manufacturers title. On the track, although beaten for the outright title, Escort Twin – Cams comfortably won the under – 2 – litre class from Porsche. By the end of 1969, Ford Escorts also held eight of the nine British circuit lap records in the 1.3 – litre and 1.6 – litre classes.

WORTH THE WAIT

Despite the constant coverage it received in Europe, Australian motoring publications of the time practically ignored the Escort. The model was certainly destined for Australian release, but Ford Australia seemed in no hurry. Cynics suggested that generating too much interest in the attractive newcomer might convince buyers to wait for its arrival rather than investing in an aging and dreary Cortina Mark 2.

A more likely explanation relates to Australia's fiercely protectionist attitude towards 'imported' cars. Prior to December 1968, only cars which were manufactured with 95 per cent Australian content could be sold in unlimited numbers. Other models – even those with extremely high levels of local input – had their production regulated by a quota system. In addition to protecting the Australian automotive industry, this system encouraged local manufacturers to perpetuate low standards, knowing that quota requirements guaranteed them a sizeable market share. Twenty years later, little seems to have changed.

Anticipating an easing in this draconian level of protection, Ford delayed its plans for Escort production until after the local content requirement was reduced to 85 per cent. Ford claimed that this figure would be reached within five years but it is doubtful if any Australian – built Escort model achieved this goal. On 12 March 1970, the waiting was over. In a statement headed 'New Ford Escort Is A Winner All Round', Ford Australia announced that the new car would go on sale during the following week.

AN ESCORT FOR EVERYONE

When introduced to Australia, the Escort range included a 1.1 – litre Standard model, the 'Super' with a choice of 1.1 – litre or 1.3 – litre engines and the 1.3 – litre GT. Despite the success of privately imported versions in local motor sport events, an Australian – built Twin – Cam was not released for almost three months.

During 1970, an Escort panel van was introduced, becoming popular with commercial and recreational buyers who appreciated its versatility and price advantage over the larger Holden and Falcon vans. With its extensive range of engines and optional equipment, the Escort was able to target a very broad market. Ford claimed that the new car would 'satisfy the economy – minded owner as well as the young driver and sports enthusiast'. Certainly, the Escort was competitively priced, with the 1.1 – litre Standard at $1770, the 1.3 Super at $1920 and the fully equipped GT costing $2350. By comparison, a 1.1 – litre Torana cost $1828 and the Toyota Corolla in its most basic form was $1849.

CROSS – FLOW PERFORMANCE

In all its configurations, the Escort engine enjoyed the benefits of a very efficient cross – flow cylinder head design. The 1.1 – litre version developed 40 kW at 5500 rpm with the longer stroke 1.3 producing 48 kW, and the GT, 56 kW at a strenuous 6000 rpm. With a combustion chamber cast into the piston crowns, the inlet and exhaust valves were mounted on opposite sides of the cylinder head. According to Ford, this configuration allowed a faster, cleaner flow of gas with resultant benefits for the performance and fuel economy.

In practice, the stylish and quick Escort 1.3 GT supported the claim. With a twin – choke Weber carburettor and extractor exhaust system, the GT would run to close on 160 km/h – slightly faster than the British version – and reach 100 km/h from rest in 13 seconds. Without the GT's more efficient carburettor and exhaust, the 'normal' 1.3 engine developed considerably less power and allowed the 1.3 Super to reach only 138 km/h. Its 0 – 100 km/h time was 15.5 seconds, although its fuel consumption at around 8.3 L/100 km was 15 per cent better than for the GT.

UPGRADED INTERIORS

Thanks more to the demands of Australia's design rules than Ford's generosity, Australian Escorts were better equipped than the UK equivalents.

Even the 1.1 – litre Standard came with a two – speed heater/demister, foot – operated windscreen washers and a door – activated interior light. On Super models, the equipment level improved considerably and included a woodgrained dash panel, carpeted interior, armrests front and rear and woven PVC seat trim. On GTs, additional instruments, driving lights, special wheel covers and 'Super Roo' decals helped justify the additional cost, but a radio was still an optional extra.

ON THE ROAD

Light weight, rack – and – pinion steering and reasonably sophisticated suspension helped the Escort to quickly establish a reputation for sporty handling. Although the wheel rims were ridiculously narrow and all but the GT ran on skinny crossply tyres, the cars were responsive and behaved well under most conditions.

Motoring journalists were impressed by the Escort's grip on dry roads but less happy with its unpredictability on wet or gravel surfaces, where smart reactions were necessary to control the rear end. But, as the Escort's string of rally victories had proven, this trait was no disadvantage in skilled hands and owners could change the car's characteristics markedly simply by fitting wider wheels with decent rubber. Standard and Super models with the 1.1 – litre engine had to manage with drum brakes all round, but discs were mandatory with the 1.3 – litre power plant and were standard on the GT models.

ENTER THE TWIN – CAM

In June 1970, the long – awaited Escort Twin – Cam hit the Australian market but brought more disappointment than excitement. The early cars were criticised for being badly built, sparsely equipped and too expensive. But, worst of all, they weren't particularly fast.

Despite a light weight and plenty of noise from the extractor exhaust system, the Twin – Cam struggled to better 170 km/h and was only marginally quicker through the gears than the more civilised and cheaper Holden Torana GTR. Up against the more powerful XU1 Toranas and rotary – engined Mazdas, the Twin – Cam also found life hard in the bump and grind of Australian production car racing. In the annual Bathurst 1000, even a class victory eluded the Escort until 1972 when a 1600GT driven by Geoff Leeds and Digby Cooke led home two Mazdas in Class B.

The Escort fared better in rallying, but its nemesis remained the Torana XU1. Even as the Holden's dominance faded towards the mid – 1970s, other challenges appeared from Nissan and Mitsubishi. The factory – backed RS1800 BDA of Greg Carr had to battle very hard to take the 1977 Australian Rally Championship.

THE OPTIONS GAME

As with Ford's larger cars, there was no shortage of options for Escort buyers. The top – selling 1300 Super came in a choice of manual and automatic transmissions while all models except the Standard could be ordered with quartz iodine driving lights, a chrome exterior mirror or full GS Rally Pack. In addition to the QI lights, special wheel covers and colour – keyed rear – view mirrors, the GS pack offered rally striping, a wooden gearlever knob and – quoting from the Ford brochure – 'the sweet, throaty purr of a Power Growl Muffler'. Heady stuff in 1970!

ONWARD AND UPWARD

In 1972 came the first in a series of changes to the Escort's model designations, the disappearance of the slow – selling 1100 Standard and 1300GT models and the replacement of the Twin – Cam by the 1600GT.

Most significantly, 1972 also saw Ford introduce a four – door version of the Escort. Two trim levels were offered, in models designated 'L' and 'XL'. Both had optional auto transmission, but only the 'XL' came with four doors. Niceties like a woodgrained dash, armrests, rear ashtrays and an interior bonnet release were now standard on the 'L' model, even though items like carpet and a radio remained optional. Buyers of the new 'Extra Luxury' model were treated to carpet, push – button radio, two – speed wipers, rubber – faced bumper overriders and chrome wheel trims. Yet, even with this dose of luxury, the prices of the Escort line – up began well below $2500.

SPORTY ESCORTS FOR ROAD AND RALLY

While the Australian sales of the Twin – Cam and 1600GT were slow, British buyers were ensuring that the products of Ford's AVO (Advanced Vehicle Operations) swiftly found homes. The first RS (standing for Rallye Sport) Escort appeared in 1970. Named RS1600, this purpose – built competition machine used a 16 – valve Cosworth – developed cylinder head and delivered over 90 kW in standard form.

Undoubtedly the biggest difference between the RS1600 and the Twin – Cam was in durability. The entire RS body structure, suspension and mechanical components were specially strengthened to cope with further modifications and the stresses of international rallying.

Following victory in the 1970 London – to – Mexico World Cup rally, Ford introduced a commemorative road – going model – appropriately named the 'Mexico'. In place of the expensive and complex 'BDA' – standing for Belt Drive Anglia – engine fitted to competition models, the Mexico used the same 1.6 – litre overhead valve power plant as the Cortina GT. While lacking the outright performance of an RS1600, the Mexico was easier to drive, cheaper to maintain and its price was within the budget of countless Escort enthusiasts.

In 1973, the first RS2000 was produced. Using the 2 – litre overhead camshaft engine developed for Ford's American 'Pinto' model, the RS2000 was a rapid road machine in the mould of the Twin – Cam and RS models, yet it delivered its performance reliably and without undue complexity.

During the 1970s, Ford Australia imported two batches of RS2000 models, mainly to qualify them for touring car racing. The first shipment arrived in 1974 and consisted of Mark 1 – bodied cars, while the second group comprised Mark 2 models with polyurethane nose cones and twin – choke Weber carburettors. They should not be confused with the locally manufactured RS2000 models built during 1979 and 1980.

HELLO, MY NAME IS BRENDA

By 1972, Escort sales had topped two million worldwide but the rapidly expanding Japanese car industry was pressuring traditional European manufacturers to significantly lift their games to stay competitive.

Under the direction of senior designer Uwe Bahnsen, Ford's German – based design unit began working on an all – new Escort. While retaining the traditional Escort values of simplicity and economy, the new model needed to tackle the Japanese head – on with greater engineering sophistication and a wider range of standard equipment. Codenamed 'Brenda', the redesigned car was similar in size to the existing model but used its dimensions more effectively. It offered 1.1 – litre, 1.3 – litre and 1.6 – litre versions of Ford's OHV 'Kent' engine – with space to fit the larger 'Pinto' motor – and uprated suspension and braking systems.

Since poor visibility was a major criticism of the previous model, Ford's Cologne designers incorporated 23 per cent more glass area into the Escort Mark 2. Next came comfort and ergonomics, with a completely new seat design and steering column – mounted stalks to control the lights, wiper/washer operation and horn. Pioneers of the 'flow through' ventilation system, Ford extended its effectiveness in the new Escort by separating the demisting system from the passenger ventilation and allowing the dash – mounted 'eyeball' vents to be used as side window demisters if required.

A LITTLE BIT OF EUROPE IN AUSTRALIA

Billed as 'The European Formula', the new Escort was announced by Ford Australia on 30 September 1975 and sales commenced in early October. Highlighting its European heritage, the brochure promoting the new model was filled with photographs of German autobahn, snow – covered peaks and Bavarian castles. Not a football, kangaroo or meat pie to be seen.

The new Escort was available in three specification levels – 'L', 'XL' and the luxurious Ghia. The XL was produced in two – door and four – door body types, with the Ghia available only as a four – door. The basic 'L' was built as a two – door.

In appearance, the Escort Mark 2 was cleaner and more angular than its predecessor. Gone were the dated 'Coke – bottle' bulge in the rear mudgaurds, the 'dog – bone' grille and rectangular headlamps. Instead, the Mark 2 had a low – waisted profile and a sharply raked rear window which merged into the boot line. Wraparound taillamps were fitted, with rubber – faced bumpers on XL and Ghia models. The headlamps on L and XL Mark 2s were round, while the Ghia looked very stylish with its square quartz halogen lights. To minimise the effects of the sun on rear seat passengers and interior trim, the rear window on all sedans was tinted, while Ghia models received tinted side glass and a tinted laminated windscreen as standard equipment.

BIGGER ENGINE AND A NEW TRANSMISSION

While the 1.3 – litre 'Kent' engine remained unchanged and the troublesome 1600GT was not replaced, the rapid performance was still available to buyers of the Ghia.

Fitted with a twin – choke Weber carburettor, the 1.6 – litre Ghia engine was lifted straight from the last of Ford's Cortina GTs. It developed 62 kW and 137 Nm of torque while returning fuel economy figures of better than 10 L/100 km. At 950 kg, the Ghia was heavier than any previous Escort – and most of its 1.6 – litre competitors – yet an auto model could reach 158 km/h and accelerate from rest to 100 km/h in 13 seconds.

Much of the new auto Escort's smoothness and willing performance was attributable to the new C – 3 'Bordeaux' automatic transmission. Ford claimed the C – 3 to be the product of three years' development and nearly five million kilometres of testing. Engineered to complement the smaller engines in Ford's range, the C – 3 was lighter, smaller and more efficient than previous auto – boxes fitted to Ford products. The C – 3 also incorporated a device which helped the transmission fluid to attain its operating temperature faster, thereby improving response and minimising component wear.

MORE SPACE, MORE FEATURES...ALL STANDARD

Although its overall dimensions varied only marginally from the Mark 1 model, the Escort Mark 2 had more rear leg room, larger door openings and a bigger boot. All models in the range also came with significantly higher levels of standard equipment than before. Priced at around $3600, even the basic 'L' model had carpets and reclining bucket seats, larger 244 mm disc front brakes, two – speed wipers with electric washers, radial ply tyres and door – mounted armrests as standard.

For an extra $400, Escort buyers could upgrade to an 'XL' model with even more interior goodies and external embellishments. The grille and door sill panels were blacked out, and upgraded seat material, an AM radio and heated rear window were added.

Those wanting a 'miniature Fairlane' had to outlay $4531 – around the price of a basic Falcon – but received a list of equipment almost as long as the car. The Escort Ghia came with its seats fully trimmed in cloth, woodgrain panelling on the dashboard, carpeted kick panels on the doors, a remote – control door mirror, carpeted boot, clock, push – button radio and a comprehensive list of other minor upgradings. Apart from a few low – volume imports, the Ghia was probably the best – equipped small car of its time sold in Australia and spurred even Japanese manufacturers to upgrade the equipment levels of competing models.

NEW VANS AS WELL

In November 1975, a new range of Escort vans with the updated 'European look' was introduced. Available in 'L' and 'XL' trim, they shared the sedans' front – end styling, plus extra soundproofing and a larger range of standard and optional equipment. Initially, the vans were only available with the 1.3 – litre engine, but a GS pack with sports wheels, driving lights, split front bumper and side striping helped to generate sales in the growing youth market.

LOWER POLLUTION... YES. MORE POWER...?

From 1 July 1976, all new cars sold in Australia were required to comply with more stringent anti – pollution measures than ever before. For most cars, compliance with Australian Design Rule 27A meant a significant power loss and this was most keenly noticed in small – engined models like the Escort 1.3.

Due to its increased weight, the Escort Mark 2 in 1.3 – litre form was widely criticised for having less performance than the previous model. Any further downgrading would have been catastrophic for sales, so Ford moved swiftly to standardise a 1.6 – litre engine across the model range.

Released early in July 1976, the 1.6 – litre Escort developed 46.5 kW at 5000 rpm and 110 Nm of torque at a low 2500 rpm. However, when the specifications for this engine and the previous 1.3 – litre were compared, some curious inconsistencies emerged. Supporting its claims that the 'emissionised' 1.6 – litre engine was more powerful than the pre – ADR 1.3, Ford stated that the 1.3 – litre engine developed 'approximately 42 kW of power'. Yet a quick comparison with the figures quoted when the Mark 2 was released shows the 1.3 engine was rated at 65 bhp or 48.7 kW.

Certainly, performance figures posted by the 'clean' 1.6 were not significantly better than those for a 'dirty' 1.3. With the smaller engine, a Mark 2 Escort would cover the standing 400 metres in 21.3 seconds, while the 1.6 – litre version was less than a second faster at 20.5 seconds. The bigger engine's benefits became most apparent in the higher speed ranges and when overtaking. Here its added torque made a considerable difference to the acceleration and the top speed in each gear.

The biggest loser in the changeover was the Escort Ghia 1.6 and the biggest winners were buyers of pre – emission Ghias. While the engine in 'dirty' form developed over 60 kW, Ghias sold after July 1976 dropped a massive 15.5 kW and their performance was seriously curtailed.

A PACK FOR EVERY OCCASION

With the 1.6 – litre engine now standard across the Escort range, Ford began to re – emphasise the car's sportier attributes.

One such model was the Escapee, a two – door 'L' model sedan with manual transmission. It was introduced in October 1976 with a dress – up package which included body side, bonnet and boot lid stripes, a rear spoiler, special paint, sports wheels with wider – section steel radials, a laminated windscreen, colour – coordinated wheel domes and the GS pack. Priced at $4546, the Escapee cost around the same as a Ghia and was aimed at younger buyers who wanted a distinctively different Escort.

THE SPORTING HERITAGE GROWS

The big news for Escort enthusiasts during 1976 was Ford Australia's decision to import a limited number of revised RS2000 models. These cars used the Mark 2 body with a sloping nose cone made from polyurethane, four quartz iodine headlamps and an integrated airdam. The boot lid featured a rubber spoiler.

Specifically imported to qualify the Escort for under – 3 – litre touring car racing, only 25 of these 'Pinto' engined cars were imported and they were snapped up by racing and rally drivers. Ford had already enjoyed success with a previous run of imported RS2000 Mark 1 models and was justifiably confident that the new cars would make the exercise equally worthwhile.

In the 1976 James Hardie 1000, RS2000s justified Ford's confidence, finishing first and third in their class and narrowly missing a top ten placing. In the 1978 race, a similar car driven by Rod Stevens and Tony Farrell finished second in its class after a furious dice with the Alfa Romeo of Le Mans winner Derek Bell. In touring car events, the RS2000 fitted well into the role of giant – killer. In the 1978 championship, for example, Stevens' Escort finished third on points behind the Toranas of Peter Brock and Bob Morris and well ahead of the more powerful Capris and other 3 – litre class cars.

In rallying, Greg Carr and John Dawson – Damer won the 1977 Australian Rally Championship in an Escort RS1800. Similar in shape to the road – going RS2000 models, the RS1800 with its BDA engine was vastly more powerful with a body and suspension system specially strengthened for rallying. Despite this, the Escorts of Carr and team – mate Colin Bond were never entirely happy in the rougher Australian conditions and were unable to repeat their victory in subsequent years.

ENTER THE 2 – LITRE

A year after standardising the 1.6 – litre across the Escort model range, Ford announced that the long – awaited 2 – litre model would finally be introduced. This decision not only saved the Escort from a premature death in the Australian market, it produced a car which still merits consideration by performance buyers motoring on a budget.

Available as an option on the 'GL' model and standard on the Ghia, the 2 – litre developed 70 kW at 5200 rpm amd 148 Nm of torque at 3800 rpm. Working best at higher engine speeds, the 2 – litre was particularly enjoyable when linked to Ford's delightful manual transmission. The performance through the gears was appreciably better than for the 1.6 – litre, with a manual GL reaching 162 km/h and accelerating to 100 km/h in 10.5 seconds.

Other advantages of 2 – litre Escorts over their smaller – engined predecessors included a larger 55 – litre fuel tank, mounted beneath the boot floor. Not only did the bigger tank considerably increase the Escort's touring range, it also increased useable boot space by 16 per cent. With greater power and torque, the 2 – litre was fitted with a higher 3.54:1 rear axle ratio which helped maintain fuel economy without a loss in acceleration.

A NEW RANGE OF OPTIONS

With the 2 – litre came an extensive range of optional items which encouraged buyers to personalise their Escort and spend more money with the local Ford dealer. Popular among them were Volante alloy wheels, upgraded Rally Pack, sports suspension package, child harness and seat, air – conditioning and a towing pack.

The sports suspension pack – which included stiffer front springs with revised shock absorber settings, a larger front antiroll bar and the addition of a rear bar – was available on all Escort models, including the Ghia, when a 2 – litre engine was fitted. Escort vans were also available with the 2 – litre engine, but only in 'GL' and specially equipped 'Sundowner' versions. The 1.6 – litre engine remained available on all 'L' and 'GL' models.

FURTHER UPGRADING

For the first time since the 1600GT was quietly removed from the Australian market, Ford had an Escort which was truly attuned to the needs of enthusiastic drivers. To ensure that the 2 – litre effectively delivered its performance, Ford also modified the running gear to suit higher speeds and harder driving.

The standard Escort braking system was uprated to Cortina specifications and the front suspension stiffened to cope with the heavier engine. The 2 – litre also gained a larger Cortina – sized clutch, stronger differential and larger diameter exhaust system. Even the badgework reflected Ford's pride in its achievement. On Rally Pack models, the demure chrome '2.0' badge fitted to Ghia models and normal GLs was replaced by a 10 cm high decal which left passers – by in no doubt that this was the new, very fast and probably antisocial 2 – litre Escort.

VAN CRAZY

During the mid – to – late 1970s, every Aussie boy wanted a van. And the dressier the better. Following the success of its Falcon and Transit – based 'Sundowner' vans, March 1978 saw Ford apply the name to a suitably modified Escort van.

In place of the normal full – glass side windows, the Escort Sundowner had tinted 'bubble' windows plus the obligatory stripes, blacked – out bumpers, grille and window strips. Inside, the seats and door trims were finished in a 'distinctive' hound's – tooth pattern while extra instrumentation and the 'soft feel' steering wheel from the GS pack made the driver a little more comfortable and well informed.

To maximise sleeping space in the Escort's cramped load area, the front bucket seats tilted forward while the rear section was equipped with a fluorescent light, internal door release, carpeted floor and vinyl spare wheel cover. Needless to say, some owners went to even greater lengths and expense, adding items like a bar, waterbed, ceiling mirror and mini – ghetto blaster to complete their 'Sundowner' package. Standard mechanicals were the 1.6 – litre engine with manual transmission, but the 2 – litre power plant with manual or auto transmission was available at extra cost.

A FINAL FACELIFT

Nearing the end of its Australian lifespan, the Escort Mark 2 range received some minor changes to its appearance and specification. Externally, these can be identified by an all – black grille with centrally mounted 'Ford' badge, square headlamps on all models and restyled wheels. On Ghia models, the spoked sports wheels were replaced by fussily styled full wheel covers. Both GL and Ghias gained a soft – feel steering wheel and an intermittent windscreen wiper action.

SAVING THE BEST UNTIL LAST

With another fuel crisis making mincemeat of traditional Australian performance car sales, Ford Australia chose a sporty – yet – economical model as its last – ever new Escort. Using the revered RS2000 nameplate, the swansong model was based on the 2 – litre GL and available in two – door and four – door versions.

Like the 'genuine' RS2000, it was fitted with an extended polyurethane nose cone and front airdam, four headlamps and a rear spoiler. Reworked sports suspension with wider – section tyres, cloth – trimmed Scheel seats, extra instrumentation, a centre console and special striping completed the package.

Priced from $6315 in two – door form, the RS2000 was the cheapest performance sedan on the Australian market. Despite delivering no more power than a 'normal' Escort 2 – litre, roadtesters found the shovel – nosed RS used its 70 kW more effectively and was more enjoyable to drive than any previous Escort. Still, some couldn't help recalling what value the original 1300GT must have been at a list price some $4000 lower than the RS.

THE ESCORT STORY CONTINUES... BUT NOT IN AUSTRALIA

Apart from a few special versions designed to keep sales moving until the new Laser made its debut, the RS2000 was the last 'new' Australian Escort and the model was withdrawn early in 1981.

Due to Ford's links with Mazda, economies of scale and the tyranny of distance, it was inevitable that Ford Australia would choose the brilliant new Mazda 323 as the basis for its new small car rather than produce its own version of the new European Escort. Compared side by side, there is little to choose between the Mazda – based Laser and the

Escort Mark 3. Both are similar in size, with the Escort's more pronounced tailgate the only major difference.

Like previous Escorts, the Mark 3 offered engines ranging in size from 1.1 to 1.6 litres and a huge variety of options. Most interesting among these − and a car most sadly missed by local Escort enthusiasts − was the XR3. This 1.6−litre two−door was a fireball in the RS2000 mould, developing the same 70 kW as the superseded Australian 2−litre cars but in a lighter, more aerodynamic body. In its earliest form, the XR3 would reach 182 km/h and, thanks to fully independent suspension and front−wheel drive, was hailed by British testers as the best−handling Escort ever.

During the mid−1980s, as convertibles re−established their popularity and overcame concerns about rigidity and safety, a cabriolet version of the XR3 was also produced in Europe. Thanks to continuing development of the 1.6−litre engine, the performance remained on a par with the more aerodynamic sedan, with improved ride, handling and undoubted style.

At the time of writing, a Mark 4 version of the Escort is on the drawing board, scheduled for release early in the 1990s. It probably won't be seen in Australia, but will continue the success of the Escort name into the 21st century.

THE GREAT SURVIVOR

The Escort's popularity can be attributed to many factors, but the most obvious are its durability and value for money. In the used car market, Escort 2−litre models have maintained their new car prices, with well−maintained Ghia and RS2000 models showing signs of appreciation. Even in the lower price ranges, a used Escort GL or one of the rare 1300GT models will provide enjoyment, strength and reasonable reliability with a touch of European style.

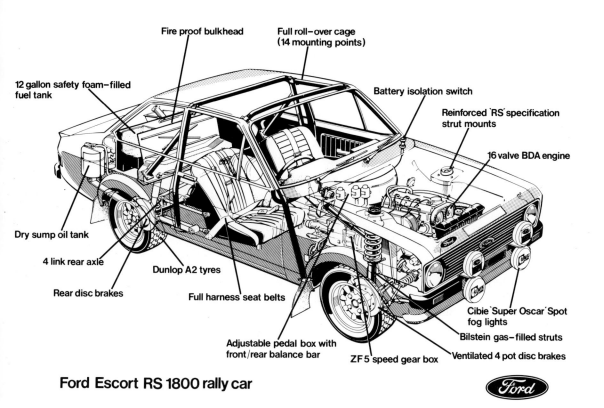

Ford Escort RS 1800 rally car

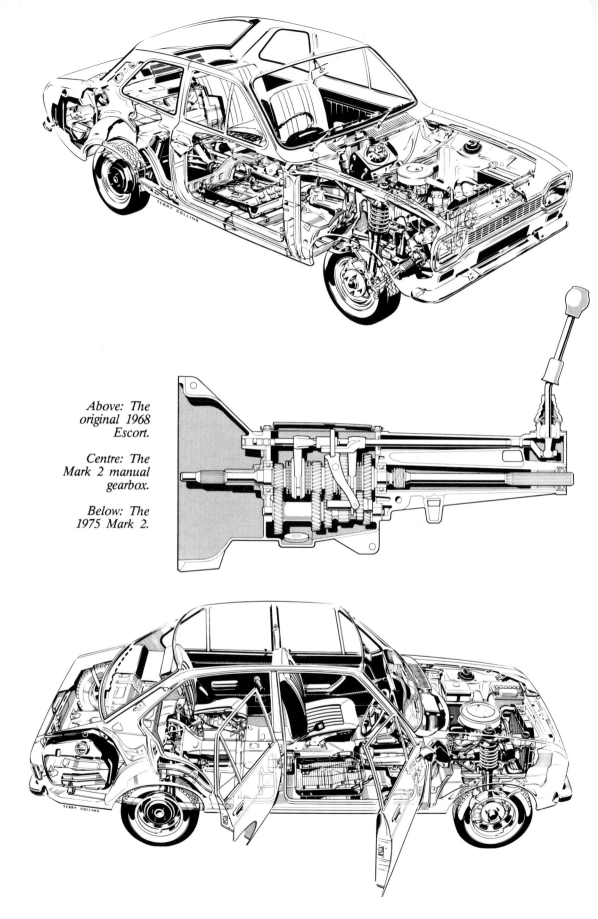

Above: The original 1968 Escort.

Centre: The Mark 2 manual gearbox.

Below: The 1975 Mark 2.

SPECIFICATIONS

+-------------------------------------+
| **MODEL:** |
| Ford Escort Mark 1 |
+-------------------------------------+

DATE OF INTRODUCTION:
20 March 1970 (with Twin – Cam following in May 1970 and panel van circa November 1970)

VEHICLE TYPE:
Two – door sedan, four – door sedan, two – door panel van

MODEL LINE – UP:
1100 Standard & Super, 1300 Standard & Super, 1300GT, 1600 Twin – Cam, 1100 & 1300 panel van

ENGINES (WITH SPECIFICATIONS):

Type: Ford – built '1100' conventional four – cycle engine
Number of cylinders: Four
Configuration: In – line
Head design: Overhead valve cross – flow
Fuel system: Single choke downdraft carburettor
Bore and stroke: 80.98 mm by 53.29 mm
Displacement: 1.089 litres
Power output (DIN): 53 bhp (40kW) at 5500 rpm
Torque (DIN): 62 lb/ft (83.7 Nm) at 3000 rpm
Compression ratio: 9:1

Type: Ford – built '1300' conventional four – cycle engine
Number of cylinders: Four
Configuration: In – line
Head design: Overhead valve cross – flow
Fuel system: Single choke downdraft carburettor
Bore and stroke: 80.98 mm by 62.99 mm
Displacement: 1.298 litres
Power output (DIN): 61.5 bhp (46 kW) at 5000 rpm
Torque (DIN): 75.5 lb/ft (98 Nm) at 2500 rpm
Compression ratio: 9:1

Type: Ford – built '1300GT' conventional four – cycle engine
Number of cylinders: Four
Configuration: In – line
Head design: Overhead valve cross – flow
Fuel system: Twin choke downdraft carburettor
Bore and stroke: 80.98 mm by 62.99 mm
Displacement: 1.298 litres
Power output (DIN): 75 bhp (56 kW) at 6000 rpm
Torque (DIN): 74.5 lb/ft (100 Nm) at 4300 rpm
Compression ratio: 9.2:1

Type: Ford – built '1600 Twin – Cam' conventional four – cycle engine
Number of cylinders: Four
Configuration: In – line
Head design: Twin overhead camshaft cross – flow
Fuel system: Dual twin choke sidedraft carburettor
Bore and stroke: 82.55 mm by 72.75 mm
Displacement: 1.558 litres
Power output (DIN): 115 bhp (86 kW) at 6000 rpm (Twin – Cam)
Torque (DIN): 116.5 lb/ft (175 Nm) at 4500 rpm (Twin – Cam)
Compression ratio: 9.5:1

TRANSMISSIONS (WITH RATIOS):

Type: Four – speed manual (1100 & 1300)
1st: 3.66:1
2nd: 2.19:1
3rd: 1.43:1
4th: 1.00:1
Reverse: 4.26:1

Type: Four – speed manual (1300GT)
1st: 3.34:1
2nd: 2.00:1
3rd: 1.42:1
4th: 1.00:1
Reverse: 4.25:1

Type: Four – speed manual (Twin – Cam)
1st: 2.97:1
2nd: 2.01:1
3rd: 1.40:1
4th: 1.00:1
Reverse: n/a

Type: Three – speed automatic
1st: 2.39:1
2nd: 1.45:1
3rd: 1.00:1
Reverse: 2.09:1

REAR AXLE RATIOS:
3.90:1 (1100 & 1300 automatic & manual); 4.12:1 (1300GT); 3.77:1 (Twin – Cam)

ENGINE/TRANSMISSION COMBINATIONS:
1100 – manual only; 1300 – manual & automatic; 1300GT – manual only; Twin – Cam – manual only

PERFORMANCE WHEN NEW:

Model: 1300 Super
Engine: 1.298 – litre, single choke
Final drive: 3.9:1
Top speeds in gears:
1st (3.66:1): 28 mph (45 km/h)
2nd (2.19:1): 48 mph (77 km/h)
3rd (1 43:1): 68 mph (109 km/h)
4th (1.00:1): 85 mph (137 km/h)
Elapsed time 0 – 100 km/h: 16.1 seconds
Standing 400 metres: 19.9 seconds

Model: Twin – Cam
Engine: 1.558 – litre, twin overhead camshaft
Final drive: 3.77:1
Top speeds in gears:
1st (2.97:1): 38 mph (61 km/h)
2nd: (2.01:1): 58 mph (93 km/h)
3rd: (1.40:1): 85 mph (136 km/h)
4th: (1.00:1): 105 mph (168 km/h)
Elapsed time 0 – 100 km/h: 9.8 seconds
Standing 400 metres: 17.0 seconds

CHASSIS/CONSTRUCTION:
Unitary/all steel

CLUTCH:
Single dry plate, diaphragm spring, mechanical actuation

SUSPENSION:
* Front: Independent with MacPherson struts and antiroll torsion bar
* Rear (with axle type): Live axle with semi-elliptic springs. Twin radius arms on GT and Twin – Cam

STEERING:
Unassisted rack – and – pinion (all models)

BRAKES:
* Front: 8 inch/203 mm diameter drums (1100); 8.6 inch/215 mm diameter discs (1300 & 1300GT); 9.6 inch/244 mm diameter discs (Twin – Cam)
* Rear: 8 inch/203 mm diameter drums (1100, 1300, 1300GT); 9 inch/229 mm diameter drums (Twin – Cam)
* Total swept area: 150.8 square inches/973 square cm (1100); 218.0 square inches/1406 square cm (1300 & 1300GT)

ELECTRICAL:
12 volt generator. 12 volt 40 amp/hr battery

IGNITION SYSTEM:
Coil and distributor

EXHAUST SYSTEM:
Standard single outlet (1100 & 1300); extractors & single outlet (1300GT & Twin – Cam)

WHEELS:
4JJ by 12 steel (1100 & 1300); 4.5JJ by 12 steel (1300GT); 5JJ by 12 steel (Twin – Cam); 5JJ by 13 alloy optional (Twin – Cam)

TYRES:
5.50 by 12 crossply (1100 & 1300 Standard & Super); 155 by 12 textile radial (1300GT); 165 by 12 textile radial (Twin – Cam); 165 by 13 textile radial optional (Twin – Cam)

INSTRUMENTS/CONTROLS:
* (Standard & Super): Speedometer/odometer/water temperature gauge, fuel gauge, oil pressure & generator warning lights
* (GT & Twin – Cam): As for Super plus tachometer, ammeter and oil pressure gauge

SEATING:
Front bucket seats/rear bench (all models)

INTERIOR DIMENSIONS:
Front leg room: 27 inches/686 mm
Rear leg room: 8.25 inches/210 mm
Front headroom: 41 inches/1042 mm
Rear headroom: 36.75 inches/934 mm
Front shoulder room: 49.75 inches/126 mm
Rear shoulder room: 49.25 inches/1251 mm
Front hip room: 52.5 inches/1336 mm
Rear hip room: 50 inches/1270 mm

EXTERIOR DIMENSIONS:
Total length: 156.6 inches/3978 mm
Total width: 61.8 inches/1635 mm
Total height at kerb weight: 53 inches/1346 mm
Wheelbase: 94.5 inches/2400 mm
Front track: 49 inches/1245 mm
Rear track: 50 inches/1270 mm
Kerb weight: 1760 lb/800 kg (1100 Standard); 1776 lb/807 kg (1300 Standard); 1775 lb/807 kg (1100 Super); 1791 lb/814 kg (1300 Super); 1780 lb/809 kg (1300GT); 1820 lb/830 kg (Twin – Cam)
Turning circle kerb to kerb: 28.75 feet/8.76 metres
Fuel tank capacity: 9 gal/40.5 litres (all models)
Cargo capacity (litres) SAE: 15 cubic feet/425 cubic decimetres

PRICES AT TIME OF INTRODUCTION:
1100 Standard: $1770
1300 Standard: $1860
1100 Super: $1920
1300 Super: $2010
1300GT: $2350
Twin – Cam: $3052

TOTAL NUMBER BUILT:
See production list at end.

MODEL:
Ford Escort Mark 1 (update)

DATE OF INTRODUCTION:
1971

VEHICLE TYPE:
Two – door sedan, four – door sedan, two – door panel van

MODEL LINE – UP:
1300L two – door, 1300XL two – door, 1300XL four – door, 1300 panel van.

ENGINES (WITH SPECIFICATIONS)

Type: Ford – built '1300' conventional four – cycle engine
Number of cylinders: Four
Configuration: In – line
Head design: Overhead valve cross – flow
Fuel system: Single choke downdraft carburettor
Bore and stroke: 80.98 mm by 62.99 mm (1300)
Displacement: 1.298 litres
Power output (DIN): 65 bhp (48.7 kW) at 5000 rpm
Torque (DIN): 74 lb/ft (100 Nm) at 3000 rpm
Compression ratio: 9:1

TRANSMISSIONS (WITH RATIOS)

Type: Four – speed manual.
1st: 3.66:1
2nd: 2.19:1
3rd: 1.43:1
4th: 1.00:1
Reverse: 4.26:1

Type: Three – speed automatic.
1st: 2.39:1
2nd: 1.45:1
3rd: 1.00:1
Reverse: 2.09:1

REAR AXLE RATIOS:
3.90:1 (1100 & 1300, automatic and manual)

ENGINE/TRANSMISSION COMBINATIONS:
1300 – manual and automatic

PERFORMANCE WHEN NEW:

Model: 1300 Super
Engine: 1.298 – litre, single choke
Final drive: 3.9:1
Top speeds in gears:
1st (3.66:1): 28 mph (45 km/h)
2nd (2.19:1): 48 mph (77 km/h)
3rd (1.43:1): 68 mph (109 km/h)
4th (1.00:1): 85 mph (137 km/h)
Elapsed time 0 – 100 km/h: 16.1 seconds
Standing 400 metres: 19.9 seconds

CHASSIS/CONSTRUCTION:
Unitary/all steel

CLUTCH:
Single dry plate, diaphragm spring, mechanical actuation

SUSPENSION:
* Front: Independent with MacPherson struts and antiroll torsion bar
* Rear (with axle type): Live axle with semi – elliptic springs.

STEERING:
Unassisted rack – and – pinion

BRAKES:
* Front: 8.6 inch/218 mm diameter discs
* Rear: 8 inch/203 mm diameter drums
* Total swept area: 218.0 square inches/1425 square cm

ELECTRICAL:
12 volt generator, 12 volt 40 amp/hr battery

IGNITION SYSTEM:
Coil and distributor

EXHAUST SYSTEM:
Standard single outlet

WHEELS:
4.5JJ by 12 steel

TYRES:
6.20 by 12 crossply (155 by 12 textile radial optional)

INSTRUMENTS/CONTROLS:
(Standard & Super): Speedometer/odometer/water temperature gauge, fuel gauge, oil pressure & generator warning lights

SEATING:
Front bucket seats/rear bench (all models)

INTERIOR DIMENSIONS:
Front leg room: 27 inches/686 mm
Rear leg room: 8.25 inches/210 mm
Front headroom: 41 inches/1042 mm
Rear headroom: 36.75 inches/934 mm
Front shoulder room: 49.75 inches/1264 mm
Rear shoulder room: 49.25 inches/1251 mm
Front hip room: 52.5 inches/1336 mm
Rear hip room: 50 inches/1270 mm

EXTERIOR DIMENSIONS:
Total length: 156.6 inches/3978 mm
Total width: 61.8 inches/1635 mm
Total height at kerb weight: 53 inches/1346 mm
Wheelbase: 94.5 inches/2400 mm
Front track: 49 inches/1245 mm
Rear track: 50 inches/1270 mm
Kerb weight: 1776 lb/807 kg (1300L); 1791 lb/814 kg (1300 Super)
Turning circle kerb to kerb: 30 feet/9.1 metres
Fuel tank capacity: 9 gal/40.5 litres (all models)
Cargo capacity (litres) SAE: 15 cubic feet/424.5 cubic decimetres

PRICES AT TIME OF INTRODUCTION:
1300L: $1925
1300XL: $2040
1300GT: $2461
Twin – Cam: $3126

TOTAL NUMBER BUILT:
See production list at end.

MODEL:
Ford Escort Mark 2

DATE OF INTRODUCTION:
6 October 1975

VEHICLE TYPE:
Two – door sedan, four – door sedan, two – door panel van

MODEL LINE – UP:
1.3 L two – door, 1.3 XL two – door, 1.3 XL four – door, 1.6 Ghia four – door, 1.3 L panel van, 1.3 XL panel van

ENGINES (WITH SPECIFICATIONS)

Type: Ford – built '1300' conventional four – cycle engine
Number of cylinders: Four
Configuration: In – line
Head design: Overhead valve cross – flow
Fuel system: Single choke downdraft carburettor
Bore and stroke: 80.98 mm by 62.99 mm
Displacement: 1.298 litres
Power output (DIN): 65 bhp (48.75 kW) at 5700 rpm
Torque (DIN): 74 lb/ft (100 Nm) at 3000 rpm
Compression ratio: 9:1

Type: Ford – built '1600' conventional four – cycle engine
Number of cylinders: Four
Configuration: In – line
Head design: Overhead valve cross – flow
Fuel system: Single twin choke downdraft carburettor
Bore and stroke: 80.98 mm by 77.62 mm
Displacement: 1.598 litres
Power output (DIN): 98 bhp (75 kW) at 6000 rpm
Torque (DIN): 101 lb/ft (136.35) at 4000 rpm
Compression ratio: 9:1

TRANSMISSIONS (WITH RATIOS)

Type: Four – speed manual
1st: 3.65:1
2nd: 1.97:1
3rd: 1.37:1
4th: 1.00:1
Reverse: 3.66:1

Type: Three – speed automatic
1st: 2.47:1
2nd: 1.47:1
3rd: 1.00:1
Reverse: 3.66:1

REAR AXLE RATIOS:
3.89:1 (manual and automatic)

ENGINE/TRANSMISSION COMBINATIONS:
1.3 – manual and automatic; 1.6 – manual & automatic

PERFORMANCE WHEN NEW:

Model: 1.3 XL
Engine: 1.298 – litre, single choke
Final drive: 3.89:1
Top speeds in gears:
1st (3.65:1): 30 mph (48 km/h)
2nd (1.97:1): 55 mph (88 km/h)
3rd (1.37:1): 79 mph (127 km/h)
4th: (1.00:1): 88 mph (142 km/h)
Elapsed time 0 – 100 km/h: 17.5 seconds (est.)
Standing 400 metres: 21.3 seconds

Model: Ghia four – door
Engine: 1.6 – litre, two – barrel (auto)
Final drive: 3.54:1
Top speeds in gears (held):
1st (2.47:1): 45 mph (72 km/h)
2nd (1.47:1): 75 mph (120 km/h)
3rd (1.00:1): 99 mph (159 km/h)
Elapsed time 0 – 100 km/h: 13.1 seconds
Standing 400 metres: 19.2 seconds

CHASSIS/CONSTRUCTION:
Unitary/all steel

CLUTCH:
Single dry plate, diaphragm spring, mechanical actuation

SUSPENSION:
* Front: Independent with MacPherson struts and anti – roll torsion bar
* Rear (with axle type): Live axle with semi – elliptic springs

STEERING:
Unassisted rack – and – pinion

BRAKES:
* Front: 9.6 inch/244 mm diameter discs
* Rear: 8 inch/203 mm diameter drums

ELECTRICAL:
12 volt alternator, 12 volt 46 amp/hr battery

IGNITION SYSTEM:
Coil and distributor

EXHAUST SYSTEM:
Standard single outlet

WHEELS:
4.5JJ by 13 steel (1.3); 5.0JJ by 13 steel (1.6)

TYRES:
155SR by 13 radial (1.3); YR78S by 13 steel radial (Ghia & optional on other models)

INSTRUMENTS/CONTROLS:
1.3 L & XL: Speedometer/odometer/water temperature gauge, fuel gauge, oil pressure & alternator warning lights
Ghia: As for XL plus tachometer, electric clock

SEATING:
Front bucket seats/rear bench (all models)

INTERIOR DIMENSIONS:
Front leg room: 40.7 inches/1034 mm
Rear leg room: 31 inches/787 mm
Front headroom: 38 inches/965 mm
Rear headroom: 36.9 inches/937 mm
Front shoulder room: 49.7 inches/1262 mm
Rear shoulder room: 49.7 inches/1262 mm
Front hip room: 52.5 inches/1336 mm
Rear hip room: 50 inches/1270 mm

EXTERIOR DIMENSIONS:
Total length: 156.6 inches/3978 mm
Total width: 62.8 inches/1595 mm
Total height at kerb weight: 54.5 inches/1384 mm
Wheelbase: 94.5 inches/2400 mm
Front track: 49.5 inches/1257 mm
Rear track: 50.5 inches/1283 mm
Kerb weight: 878 kg (1.3 L); 884 kg (1.3 XL two – door); 909 kg (1.3 XL four – door): 950 kg (1.6 Ghia)
Turning circle kerb to kerb: 29.2 feet/8.9 metres
Fuel tank capacity: 9 gal/40.5 litres (all models)
Cargo capacity (litres) SAE: 10.7 cubic feet/303 decimetres

PRICES AT TIME OF INTRODUCTION:
1.3 L two – door: $3430
1.3 XL two – door: $3730
1.3 XL two – door: $3830
1.6 Ghia four – door: $4420

TOTAL NUMBER BUILT:
See production list at end.

```
+-----------------------------------------+
| MODEL:                                  |
| Ford Escort Mark 2 (ADR 27A model)      |
+-----------------------------------------+
```

DATE OF INTRODUCTION:
1 July 1976

VEHICLE TYPE:
Two – door sedan, four – door sedan, two – door panel van

MODEL LINE – UP:
1.6 L two – door, 1.6 XL two – door, 1.6 XL four – door, 1.6 Ghia four – door, 1.6 L panel van, 1.6 XL panel van

ENGINES (WITH SPECIFICATIONS):

Type: Ford – built '1600' conventional four – cycle engine
Number of cylinders: Four
Configuration: In – line
Head design: Overhead valve cross – flow
Fuel system: Single choke downdraft carburettor (all models)
Bore and stroke: 80.98 mm by 77.62 mm
Displacement: 1.598 litres
Power output (DIN): 61 bhp (46 kW) at 5000 rpm
Torque (DIN): 81 lb/ft (110 Nm) at 2500 rpm
Compression ratio: 8:1

TRANSMISSIONS (WITH RATIOS):

Type: Four – speed manual
1st: 3.65:1
2nd: 1.97:1
3rd: 1.37:1
4th: 1.00:1
Reverse: 3.66:1

Type: Three – speed automatic
1st: 2.47:1
2nd: 1.47:1
3rd: 1.00:1
Reverse: 3.66:1

REAR AXLE RATIOS:
3.77:1 (manual and automatic)

ENGINE/TRANSMISSION COMBINATIONS:
1.6 (manual and automatic)

PERFORMANCE WHEN NEW

Model: 1.6 XL
Engine: 1.598 – litre, single choke
Final drive: 3.77:1
Top speeds in gears:
1st (3.65:1): 30 mph (48 km/h)
2nd (1.97:1): 56 mph (90 km/h)
3rd (1.37:1): 80 mph (129 km/h)
4th (1.00:1): 92 mph (148 km/h)
Elapsed time 0 – 100 km/h: 18.5 seconds (est.)
Standing 400 metres: 20.5 seconds

CHASSIS/CONSTRUCTION:
Unitary/all steel

CLUTCH:
Single dry plate, diaphragm, spring, mechanical actuation

SUSPENSION:
* Front: Independent with MacPherson struts and antiroll torsion bar
* Rear (with axle type): Live axle with semi – elliptic springs

STEERING:
Unassisted rack – and – pinion

BRAKES:
Front: 9.6 inch/244 mm diameter discs
Rear: 8 inch/203 mm diameter drums

ELECTRICAL:
12 volt alternator, 12 volt 46 amp/hr battery

IGNITION SYSTEM:
Coil and distributor

EXHAUST SYSTEM:
Standard single outlet

WHEELS:
5.0JJ by 13 steel (1.6)

TYRES:
155SR by 13 radial (L & XL); YR78S by 13 steel radial (Ghia & optional other models)

INSTRUMENTS/CONTROLS:
L & XL: Speedometer/odometer/water temperature gauge, fuel gauge, oil pressure & alternator warning lights
Ghia: As for XL plus tachometer, electric clock

SEATING:
Front bucket seats/rear bench (all models)

INTERIOR DIMENSIONS
Front leg room: 40.7 inches/1034 mm
Rear leg room: 31.0 inches/787 mm
Front headroom: 38 inches/965 mm
Rear headroom: 36.9 inches/937 mm
Front shoulder room: 49.7 inches/1262 mm
Rear shoulder room: 49.7 inches/1262 mm
Front hip room: 52.5 inches/1336 mm
Rear hip room: 50 inches/1270 mm

EXTERIOR DIMENSIONS:
Total length: 156.6 inches/3978 mm
Total width: 62.8 inches/1595 mm
Total height at kerb weight: 54.5 inches/1384 mm
Wheelbase: 94.5 inches/2400 mm
Front track: 49.5 inches/1257 mm
Rear track: 50.5 inches/1283 mm
Kerb weight: 970 kg (1.6 XL two – door)
Turning circle kerb to kerb: 29.2 feet/8.9 metres
Fuel tank capacity: 9 gal/40.5 litres (all models)
Cargo capacity (litres) SAE: 10.7 cubic feet/303 cubic decimetres

PRICES AT TIME OF INTRODUCTION:
1.6 L two – door: $3891
1.6 XL two – door: $4225
1.6 XL four – door: $4337
1.6 Ghia four – door $4926
1.6 L van $3725
1.6 XL van $4032

TOTAL NUMBER BUILT:
See production list at end.

MODEL:
Ford Escort Mark 2, 2–litre

DATE OF INTRODUCTION:
1 July 1977

VEHICLE TYPE:
Two–door sedan, four–door sedan, two–door panel van

MODEL LINE–UP:
2.0 GL two–door, 2.0 GL four–door, 2.0 Ghia four–door, RS2000 two–door, RS2000 four–door, 2.0 GL panel van

ENGINES (WITH SPECIFICATIONS):
Type: Ford–built '2000' conventional four–cycle engine
Number of cylinders: Four
Configuration: In–line
Head design: Single overhead camshaft
Fuel system: Single twin choke downdraft carburettor
Bore and stroke: 90.82 mm by 76.95 mm
Displacement: 1.993 litres
Power output (DIN): 70 kW at 5200 rpm
Torque (DIN): 148 Nm at 3800 rpm
Compression ratio: 9.2:1

TRANSMISSIONS (WITH RATIOS):
Type: Four–speed manual
1st: 3.65:1
2nd: 1.97:1
3rd: 1.37:1
4th: 1.10:1
Reverse: 3.66:1

Type: Three–speed automatic
1st: 2.47:1
2nd: 1.47:1
3rd: 1.00:1
Reverse: 3.66:1

REAR AXLE RATIOS:
3.54:1 (manual and automatic)

ENGINE/TRANSMISSION COMBINATIONS:
2.0 (manual and automatic)

PERFORMANCE WHEN NEW:

Model: 2.0 GL two–door
Engine: 1.993–litre, twin choke
Final drive: 3.54:1
Top speeds in gears:
1st (3.65:1): 41 km/h
2nd (1.97:1): 82 km/h
3rd (1.37:1): 129 km/h
4th (1.10:1): 162 km/h
Elapsed time 0–100 km/h: 11.2 seconds
Standing 400 metres: 18.0 seconds

Model: RS2000
Engine: 1.993–litre, twin choke
Final drive: 3.54:1
Top speeds in gears:
1st (3.65:1): 41 km/h
2nd (1.97:1): 82 km/h
3rd (1.37:1): 130 km/h
4th (1.10:1): 168 km/h
Elapsed time 0–100 km/h: 11.0 seconds
Standing 400 metres: 17.9 seconds

CHASSIS/CONSTRUCTION:
Unitary/all steel

CLUTCH:
Single dry plate, diaphragm spring, mechanical actuation

SUSPENSION:
* Front: Independent with Macpherson struts and antiroll torsion bar
* Rear (with axle type): Live axle with semi–elliptic springs

STEERING:
Unassisted rack–and–pinion

BRAKES:
* Front: 9.6 inch/244 mm diameter discs
* Rear: 8 inch/203 mm diameter drums

ELECTRICAL:
12 volt alternator, 12 volt 46 amp/hr battery

IGNITION SYSTEM:
Coil and distributor

EXHAUST SYSTEM:
Standard single outlet

WHEELS:
5.0JJ by 13 steel

TYRES:
155SR by 13 radial (GL); ZR78S by 13 steel radial (Ghia & optional on other models)

INSTRUMENTS/CONTROLS:
GL: Speedometer/odometer/water temperature gauge, fuel gauge, oil pressure & alternator warning lights
Ghia: As for XL plus tachometer, electric clock

SEATING:
Front bucket seats/rear bench (all models)

INTERIOR DIMENSIONS
Front leg room: 1041 mm
Rear leg room: 828 mm
Front headroom: 965 mm
Rear headroom: 937 mm
Front shoulder room: 1262 mm
Rear shoulder room: 1262 mm
Front hip room: 1336 mm
Rear hip room: 1270 mm

EXTERIOR DIMENSIONS:
Total length: 3978 mm
Total width: 1595 mm
Total height at kerb weight: 1384 mm
Wheelbase: 2400 mm
Front track: 1270 mm
Rear track: 1296 mm
Kerb weight: 925 kg (2.0 GL); 978 kg (RS2000); 1003 kg (2.0 Ghia); 908 kg (2.0 GL van)
Turning circle kerb to kerb: 8.9 metres
Fuel tank capacity: 54 litres (all models)
Cargo capacity (litres) SAE: 11.6 cubic feet

PRICES AT TIME OF INTRODUCTION:
2.0 GL two–door: $5100
2.0 GL four–door: $5226
2.0 Ghia: $5828
RS2000 two–door: $6676
RS2000 four–door: $7056
2.0 GL van: $4880

* 1970 (1970 model):
Two – door – 8057; Four – door – 2846;
Van – 1242; Total – 12,145
* 1971 (1970 model):
Two – door – 6947; Four – door – 1723;
Van – 2048; Total – 10,718
* 1972 (1970 model):
Two – door – 23; Four – door – 0;
Van – 0; Total – 23
* 1972 (1971 model):
Two – door – 6747; Four – door – 2552;
Van – 3405; Total – 12,704
* 1973 (1972 model):
Two – door – 4257; Four – door – 1740;
Van – 2827; Total – 8824
* 1973 (1973 model):
Two – door – 1066; Four – door – 556;
Van – 316; Total – 1938
* 1974 (1973 model):
Two – door – 5065; Four – door – 2449;
Van – 3564; Total – 11,078
* 1975 (1973 model):
Two – door – 4120; Four – door – 2179;
Van – 3417; Total – 9716
* 1975 (1976 model):
Two – door – 3036; Four – door – 2207;
Van – 939; Total – 6182
* 1976 (1976 model):
Two – door – 6553; Four – door – 11,051;
Van – 4975; Total – 22,579
* 1977 (1976 model):
Two – door – 751; Four – door – 2758;
Van – 1137; Total – 4646
* 1977 (1977 model):
Two – door – 2091; Four – door – 3114;
Van – 2610; Total – 7815
* 1978 (1977 model):
Two – door – 2409; Four – door – 5805;
Van – 2847; Total – 11,061
* 1978 (1979 model):
Two – door – 397; Four – door – 61;
Van – 78; Total – 536
* 1979 (1977 model):
Two – door – 0; Four – door – 282;
Van – 0; Total – 282
* 1979 (1979 model):
Two – door – 4374; Four – door – 7237;
Van – 2848; Total – 14,459
* 1980 (1979 model):
Two – door – 3237; Four – door – 5632;
Van – 2985; Total – 11,854
* 1981 (1979 model):
Two – door – 0; Four – door – 0;
Van – 289; Total – 289

* TOTALS for 1970 to 1981:
Two – door – 59,130; Four – door – 52,192;
Van – 35,527; Total – 146,849

OWNER'S DETAILS – CAR ONE

Model:

Year of Manufacture:

Body type:

Engine type:

Transmission:

Colour:

Engine number:

Chassis number:

Date purchased:

Previous owner:

       Address:

Purchase price:

Odometer reading when purchased:

Modifications/Options fitted:

Notes on previous history:

OWNER'S DETAILS – CAR TWO

Model:

Year of Manufacture:

Body type:

Engine type:

Transmission:

Colour:

Engine number:

Chassis number:

Date purchased:

Previous owner:

       Address:

Purchase price:

Odometer reading when purchased:

Modifications/Options fitted:

Notes on previous history:

Ford ESCORT 1970-75

MODEL CODE

CODE	BODY TYPE		YEAR RANGE
11012	'STD' Sedan	2 Door	1970
11016	'Super' Sedan	2 Door	1970
11018	'GT' Sedan	2 Door	1970
11019	'Twin Cam' Sedan	2 Door	1970
11036	'Super' Sedan	4 Door	1970
41082	'STD' Van		1970
11112	'L' Sedan	2 Door	1971
11116	'XL' Sedan	2 Door	1971
11118	'GT' Sedan	2 Door	1971
11119	'Twin Cam' Sedan	2 Door	1971
11136	'XL' Sedan	4 Door	1971
41182	'STD' Van		1971
11212	'L' Sedan	2 Door	1972
11216	'XL' Sedan	2 Door	1972
11218	'Super Luxury'	2 Door	1972
11219	'GT'	2 Door	1972
11236	'XL'	4 Door	1972
41282	'STD' Van		1972
11712	'L' Sedan	2 Door	1972½
11716	'XL' Sedan	2 Door	1972½
11717	'Super Luxury'	2 Door	1972½
11736	'XL' Sedan	4 Door	1972½
41782	'STD' Van		1972½
11312	'L' Sedan	2 Door	1973½
11316	'XL' Sedan	2 Door	1973½
11336	'XL' Sedan	4 Door	1973½
41382	'STD' Van		1973½

ENGINE CODE

CODE	TYPE
B	67 CID (1100 cc)
L	79 CID (1300 cc) 1V
T	79 CID (1300 cc) 2V
H	95 CID (1558 cc) D.O.H.C.

TRANSMISSION CODE

CODE	TYPE		
V	4-Speed		Floor Shift
X	4-Speed	Close Ratio	Floor Shift
Y	3-Speed	Automatic	Floor Shift

ENGINE

	NUMBER OF CYL.	BORE	STROKE	CAPACITY
1100	4	3.1881"	2.098"	1098 cc
1300	4	3.1881"	2.480"	1297 cc
1560	4	3.2506"	2.867"	1558 cc

SPARK PLUG

TYPE	Motorcraft
SIZE	14 mm

FIRING ORDER

1100/1300	1.2.4.3
1560	1.3.4.2

FLUID CAPACITY

ENGINE — OIL	1100/1300	3.6 litre (6.4 pts)
	1560	3.7 litre (6.5 pts) includes filter
TRANS. — OIL		
Manual		0.8 litres (1.5 pts)
Auto.		6.4 litre (11.3 pts)
REAR AXLE — OIL		1.1 litre (2.0 pts)
FUEL TANK		41.0 litre (9.0 galls)
COOLING SYSTEM		5.1 litre (9.0 pts)

Ford ESCORT 1975-81

MODEL CODE

CODE	BODY TYPE		YEAR RANGE
11612	'L' Sedan	2 Door	1975 to 6/77
11616	'XL' Sedan	2 Door	1975 to 6/77
11636	'XL' Sedan	4 Door	1975 to 6/77
11638	'Ghia' Sedan	4 Door	1975 to 6/77
41682	'L' Van		1975 to 6/77
41686	'XL' Van		1975 to 6/77
11712	'L' Sedan	1.6 litre — 2 Door	6/77 to 12/78
11716	'GL' Sedan	1.6 litre — 2 Door	6/77 to 12/78
11717	'GL' Sedan	2.0 litre — 2 Door	6/77 to 12/78
11736	'GL' Sedan	1.6 litre — 4 Door	6/77 to 12/78
11737	'GL' Sedan	2.0 litre — 4 Door	6/77 to 12/78
11739	'Ghia' Sedan	2.0 litre — 4 Door	6/77 to 12/78
41782	'L' Van	1.6 litre	6/77 to 12/78
41786	'GL' Van	1.6 litre	6/77 to 12/78
41788	'GL' Van	1.6 litre (Sundowner)	12/77 to 12/78
41787	'GL' Van	2.0 litre	6/77 to 12/78
41789	'GL' Van	2.0 litre (Sundowner)	12/77 to 12/78
11912	'L' Sedan	1.6 litre — 2 Door	12/78/-
11916	'GL' Sedan	1.6 litre — 2 Door	12/78/-
11917	'GL' Sedan	2.0 litre — 2 Door	12/78/-
11918	'RS 2000' Sedan	2.0 litre — 2 Door	5/79/-
11932	'L' Sedan	1.6 litre — 4 Door	5/78/-
11936	'GL' Sedan	1.6 litre — 4 Door	5/78/-
11937	'GL' Sedan	2.0 litre — 4 Door	12/78/-
11938	'RS 2000' Sedan	2.0 litre — 4 Door	5/79/-
11939	'Ghia' Sedan	2.0 litre — 4 Door	12/78/-
41982	'L' Van	1.6 litre	12/78/-
41986	'GL' Van	1.6 litre	12/78/-
41988	'GL' Van	1.6 litre (Sundowner)	12/78/-
41987	'GL' Van	2.0 litre	12/78/-
41989	'GL' Van	2.0 litre (Sundowner)	12/78/-

ENGINE CODE

CODE	TYPE		
L	1.3 Litre	4 Cylinder 1V	High Compression
D	1.6 Litre	4 Cylinder 2V	High Compression
E	1.6 Litre	4 Cylinder 1V	Low Compression
J	2.0 Litre	4 Cylinder 2V	High Compression
R	2.0 Litre	4 Cylinder 2V	Low Compression

TRANSMISSION CODE

CODE	TYPE		
V	4-Speed	Floor Shift	Manual
Y	3-Speed	Floor Shift	Automatic

FLUID CAPACITY

ENGINE — OIL	1.3/1.6		3.25 litre (5.7 pts)
	2.0		3.15 litre (5.5 pts) includes filter
TRANS. — OIL			
Manual			1.4 litre (2.5 pts)
Auto.			6.5 litre (11.4 pts)
REAR AXLE — OIL			1.1 litre (2.0 pts)
FUEL TANK	Sedan		36.0 litre (8.0 galls) to 6/77
	Sedan		53.0 litre (11.66 galls) from 6/77
	Van		41.0 litre (9.0 galls)
COOLING SYSTEM	1.3		5.0 litre (8.8 pts)
	1.6		5.8 litre (9.5 pts)
	2.0		7.1 litre (12.4 pts)

ENGINE

	NUMBER OF CYL.	BORE	STROKE	CAPACITY
1.3 litre	4	3.188"	2.478"	1263 cc
1.6 litre	4	3.188"	3.056"	1598 cc
2.0 litre	4	3.575"	3.03"	1993 cc

SPARK PLUG

MAKE Motorcraft	
SIZE 1.3/1.6	14 mm
2.0	18 mm

FIRING ORDER

1.3/1.6	1.2.4.3
2.0	1.3.4.2

FORD ESCORT USED CAR NOTES ADAPTED FROM 'WHICH CAR FOR YOU?'

Although the high-performance versions of Ford's Escort are exceptionally sought after, some of the the lesser models have been almost forgotten by used car buyers. Nevertheless, it would be a mistake to overlook the Escort when searching for an agreeable small car. Although the Escort was not as popular in its day as the brilliantly successful Laser which replaced it, for motorists seeking a small, low-cost, used car which is light on fuel, easy to handle and readily serviced, Escorts can make good buying.

They were assembled in Australia throughout the 1970s, the first being released in March 1970, the last being sold in early 1981. The original Escort was designed in Britain as a replacement for Ford's small postwar car, the Anglia, and is an orthodox rear-wheel drive light sedan with seating for four. It was assembled here until October 1975 when a German-derived model took its place.

The first generation Escorts were fitted with a choice between 1.1-litre (38 kW), 1.3-litre (46 kW) and 1.3-litre GT (56 kW) engines. They were available with two or four doors. The British designs, easily recognised by the dog-bone shaped radiator, came with two levels of equipment, designated Escort Standard and Super. In 1971 the Standard and Super became the X and XL models.

An all-new body style, recognised by a crisper appearance and a more conventional grille, was launched in October 1975. It has similar dimensions to the earlier Escort with extra passenger and luggage space. The main differences between the first and second designs were the additional standard equipment and the introduction of an optional 1.6-litre engine. The bigger engine was initially available only on Ghia luxury models but became standard on all Escorts in mid-1976.

In a similar manner, a 2-litre engine was introduced on the Ghia in mid-1977 and later became standard throughout the Escort range. The 2-litre model especially has a spirited performance and, though not quiet, is fun to drive.

With the revised design in July 1977, the XL was renamed GL, and given additional equipment. A larger fuel tank (55 litres) was fitted, placed under the floor to provide extra boot room. To match the increase in power, the 2-litre models have a stronger clutch, more direct axle ratio and a beefed-up front suspension.

In January 1979, a facelifted Escort was launched with L, GL and Ghia levels of trim. It can be recognised by the rectangular headlamps and all-black grille. The German-derived Escorts proved marginally more popular than the earlier models. Although they were willing and economical workhorses, they never attained the same popularity as the rival Japanese light cars. This lack of popularity is the used car buyer's gain, because good Escorts still sell for appreciably less than comparable Japanese cars.

Some Escort models, such as the sporting RS2000, fetch relatively high sums and have very good performance. Unfortunately, the insurance rates are high (particularly for young drivers), so check the policy cost before being committed.

Though primarily a four-passenger sedan, Escort can seat three small children in the back. It is a straightforward design, with a fairly roomy boot and a conventional shape. Mechanically, the design is orthodox and, when serviced correctly, reliable and durable. The car's strong points lie largely with the gearbox, clutch and engine. Fuel economy (around 7.8 litres per 100 kilometres, or 36 miles per gallon on the open road) is good and parking is easy.

The main design faults are a tendency to lock-up the rear brakes on slippery surfaces and a choppy ride on uneven road surfaces. The fresh air ventilation is limited and the rear doors do not open widely. Many of the faults which arose in early Escorts were the result of poor local assembly. Body rattles and badly fitting doors are common. Poor door fitment can cause water leaks so the entire car including the floor of the boot and passenger compartments should be scrutinised for possible rust. A common fault with two-door cars is a breakdown in the bond between the hinges and glass of the rear side windows, so open the windows and gently move them to see if the problem exists.

Provided they have been regularly serviced, the engines, gearboxes, clutch and axles generally give little trouble. The exception is the 2-litre engine, which can be subject to premature wear of the overhead camshaft and cam drive belts. Check for possible oil leaks from both manual and automatic transmissions.

Rough idling is common. The engines are hard to keep in tune, but this is not serious and does not affect long-term durability. However oil fuming and audible piston slap suggest that a major engine overhaul is due.

It is important to check the front tyres, as an unusual wear pattern may indicate problems with the MacPherson strut suspension. This fault is dear to fix. Most Escorts refuse to retain proper wheel alignment for more than about 5000 km, another cause of premature tyre wear.

Escorts - even the less fashionable models - are well designed, practical, economical to run and fun to drive.

'WHICH CAR FOR YOU? - THE AUSTRALIAN BUYER'S GUIDE TO USED CARS' (THIRD EDITION) WAS WRITTEN BY PEDR DAVIS AND PUBLISHED BY GREGORY'S IN ASSOCIATION WITH MARQUE PUBLISHING COMPANY PTY LTD.

Left: An early PR photo of the 'Anglia replacement', in this case the base 1100L version as sold in the UK.

Centre and below: A 1969 shot of the Escort GT which was never sold in Australia as a four-door.

This page: The Escort estate was passed over by Ford Australia management, although they picked up the van. This is a 1968 UK version.

Right top: An early Aussie brochure.

Right bottom: The Escort Mexico was named after the Escort had achieved success in the 1970 London – to – Mexico World Cup Rally. By 1970 total Escort sales had topped 750,000. The Australian range was launched in March that year.

Record-breaking performance...

Escort is no stranger to the tough, fiercely competitive world of motor sport where it's a survival of the fittest...where reputations are made——and broken. Escort has made it––*big!* in just 2 years it has notched up over 200 victories in European races and rallies, more than any other car!

What makes it so good? Everything about Escort: The Ford CrossFlow design engine pours out snap-to-it, step-lively power and effortless day long cruising with very little thirst for petrol.

A 4-speed, all synchromesh manual transmission, with a racy floor-mounted stick, meets all traffic or rally needs with crisp, positive short-shifts.

Rack-and-pinion steering and a small 29ft. turning circle mean precision handling and easy parkability.

Independent front suspension with Macpherson telescopic dampers, and rear suspension with double-action shock-absorbers give you a positive feeling on the road without you feeling every hole and bump.

Best of all, is the way you feel behind the wheel. Escort's superb driving position is out on its own. We can't describe it; you have to take it up yourself to know just how good driver-comfort, vision, placement of controls and instruments can be. Your road test of Escort will spell out all its virtues to you, beautifully.

Performance Specifications

'1100' AND '1300' ENGINES: 4-cylinder OHV CrossFlow Bowl-in-Piston design featuring 5 main bearing crankshaft; valves pushrod operated; mechanical

diaphragm type fuel pump; single-carburettor.
GT ENGINE: High-performance '1, engine with special high-lift camsh OHV CrossFlow Bowl-in-Piston de 2-barrel Weber carburettor.
TWIN-CAM ENGINE: A 'Hemi'. Features Lotus-designed cylinder with opposed layout; two 2-barrel carburettors; 4-branch free-flow ex system; valve operation by twin ove camshafts.
GEAR RATIOS.
Escort Sedan and Super: 1st—14.2 2nd—8.52, 3rd—5.56, 4th—3.90, —16.52
GT Sedan: 1st—13.77, 2nd—8.23, 5.85, 4th—4 13, Reverse—14 95
Twin-Cam Sedan: 1st—11.23, 2nd 3rd—5.28, 4th—3.78, Reverse—1

Above: An RS1600 from FAVO (Ford Advanced Vehicle Operations) with strengthened body, wheel arch extensions and rally equipment.

Top right: Double world champion F1 driver Graham Hill was behind the wheel for this publicity shot. The RS1600 had previously been built at Liverpool.

Bottom right: The Escort Twin – Cam, released in Australia in 1970, wore the same 'Super Roo' stickers as its big brother, the Falcon GT.

ESCORT RS 1600
ADVANCED VEHICLE OPERATIONS
FIRST PRODUCTION CAR AT AVELEY

...KES:
...ort Sedan and Super Sedan—big
...ch diameter drum brakes all round.
...ort GT — servo-assisted front disc
...es (8.6 ins. diameter), with servo-
...sted rear drum brakes (8 ins.
...meter).
...ort Twin-Cam—servo-assisted front
... brakes (9.6 ins. diameter), servo-
...sted rear drum brakes (9 ins.
...meter).
...e GT servo-assisted front disc brakes
... fitted on Escort Sedan and Super,
...n the optional '1300' engine is
...ered.)

...SPENSION:
...ort Sedan and Super: Front—
...ependent coil springs with
...scopic shock-absorbers. Rear —
...mi-elliptic springs with hydraulic
...ble-action shock-absorbers.

GT Sedan: Front—independent coil
springs with Macpherson telescopic
dampers in compliance. Rear —
semi-elliptic springs with hydraulic
double-action telescopic
shock-absorbers.
Twin-Cam Sedan: Front—independent
coils, Macpherson telescopic dampers
and stabilizer bar. Rear—special rate
springs with hydraulic double-action
shock-absorbers and 2 trailing links.

WHEELS AND TYRES:
Escort Sedan and Super: 4" wide x 12"
wheels and 5.50 x 12 tubeless tyres.
GT Sedan: 4½" wide x 12" wheels
and 155 x 12 radial ply tyres.
Twin-Cam Sedan: 5" wide x 12"
wheels and 165 x 12 radial ply tyres.
(The GT 4½" wide wheels and 155 x
12 radial ply tyres are optional on
Escort Sedan and Super.)

Engine Specifications	'1100'	'1300'	'1300' GT	'1600' Twin Cam
Displacement (cc/cu. ins)	1098/67.0	1298/79.2	1298/79.2	1560/95.2
Bore/Stroke	3.19 x 2.10	3.19 x 2.48	3.19 x 2.48	3.25 x 2.86
Max BHP @ RPM	53 @ 5500	61.5 @ 5000	75 @ 6000	115 @ 6000
Max Torque @ RPM	62 @ 3000	75.5 @ 2500	74.5 @ 4300	106 @ 4500
Compression Ratio	9.0:1	9.0:1	9.2:1	9.5:1

Above and centre: This 1971 Escort Sport was another of the myriad performance – orientated versions of the Escort. It was a UK – only model.

Below: The 1300E two – door from 1973. This luxury UK model had no Australian equivalent until the Mark 2 Ghia in 1975.

Left: The 1300E two-door from 1973.

Below: Another FAVO (Ford Advanced Vehicle Operations) effort was this 2-litre single overhead cam RS2000 from 1973.

Left: The RS2000.

Below: 1973 RS2000, in left-hand drive.

*Above: The Escort and the car it replaced: the Ford Anglia. The curiously styled Anglia was much criticised but much purchased. 1,288,956 units were sold. The Escort passed this figure in 1974, hence this Ford publicity shot.
The Australian brochure on these pages is of a late series Mark 1.*

Opposite page, top: The 'Little Ripper' van – complete with stickers of an Anzac – hatted kangaroo – was produced for the booming Australian panel van market in 1975.

Opposite page, bottom: New Mark 2 Escorts hidden at Ford Australia before the Australian release.

Little Ripper!

rand Sport Rally Pack and Options

Escort is all fun —and go. Add the GS Rally Pack (items illustrated on catalogue) and you really let it show. Up front, a pair of Quartz-Iodine long-range driving lights are built into the grille. Special chrome wheel covers set off your wheels. Raking GS Rally Stripes sweep along the side. An exterior styled rear-view mirror lets you see all that's happening behind. Inside . . . you have a padded Sports Steering Wheel.

OTHER OPTIONS. The whole idea of Escort's options is to allow you to tailor your car exactly to your needs. Choose the equipment you want from the list on the left.

Escort cares for your safety.

Escort has been engineered and built with your safety in mind. Here are the Escort Lifeguard Safety Features you get standard: Collapsible Steering Column • Safety-Styled, Heavily Padded Steering Wheel • Safety Glass in all windows • Zone-Toughened Windshield • Windshield Washers • Electric Windshield Wipers • High-speed wiper blades • Safety-Rim Wheels • Front and Rear Lap/Sash Seat Belts • 2-speed Freshflo Heater • Demister • Front and Rear Turn-Signal Lights • Headlamp Flasher • Tip Device on front seats • Safety Sun Visors • Padded Instrument Panel • Steering Column Lock • High-back front seats incorporating head restraints • Reversing Lights • Yield-away interior rear-view mirror.

Option Availability		
	Escort L	Escort XL
...bar Automatic	Opt	Opt
...ted/Laminated Windshield	Opt.	Opt.
Quartz-Iodine Long-Range Driving Lights	Opt.	Opt.
Full Wheelcovers	Opt.	Opt.
Sports Steering Wheel		Opt.
Exterior Style Mirror R/H (remote control)	Opt.	Opt.
Exterior Style Mirror L/H	Opt.	Std.
Reclining Seats	Opt.	Std.
Carpet		Opt.
Push-Button Long-Range Radio	Opt.	Std
GS Rally Pack (complete)	Opt.	Opt.
Radial Ply Tyres	Opt.	Opt.
Whitewall Tyres	Opt.	Opt.
White Roof	Opt.	Opt.
Country-Ride Suspension	Opt.	Opt.
Heavy-Duty Battery	Opt.	Opt.

Footnotes to Option Chart above: Opt.s "Opt" means optional equipment. Std means Standard Equipment

Illustrations and information presented are correct when approved for printing. Ford Motor Company of Australia Limited and/or Ford Sales Company of Australia Limited reserves the right to change at any time, the specifications or design without incurring obligations. Some features shown or described are optional at extra cost. Some colours are and required with other options. Please consult your Ford Dealer for the latest model complete information, prices, features, prices and availability.
FORD SALES COMPANY OF AUSTRALIA LIMITED, 1735 Sydney Rd., Campbellfield

FORD ESCORT

Going Ford is the going thing!

Left: The 1975 'L' two – door Australian Escort Mark 2. Ford boasted a 23 per cent increase in the glass area.

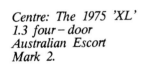

Centre: The 1975 'XL' 1.3 four – door Australian Escort Mark 2.

Left: Another view of the Australian XL model, highlighting the new ABS plastic grille.

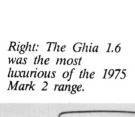

Right: The Ghia 1.6 was the most luxurious of the 1975 Mark 2 range.

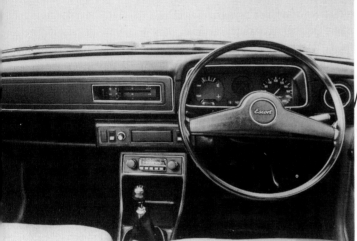

Above: Inside the Mark 2 — neat but sparse.

Below: A shot of the 1975 English Escort Popular and its 1934 predecessor, the Y- model Popular.

OPTIONS

An extensive range of new options are available to personalise the new Escort. Appearance, convenience, safety and performance items are available. The special lightweight C3 automatic transmission has been designed and built by Ford for added enjoyment of the new Escort. The complete range of options includes:—

	SEDANS			VAN	
	L	XL	GHIA	L	XL
1 C3 Automatic transmission	O	O	O	O	O
Reclining front seats	O	O	O	O	O
2 RHS door mounted remote control mirror	STD	STD	STD	N.A.	O
LHS door mounted rear view mirror	O	STD	STD	N.A.	N.A.
3 Heated rear window	O	O	STD	O	O
Sports road wheels (1)	O	STD	STD	STD	STD
Vinyl roof	N.A.	N.A.	STD	N.A.	N.A.
Van side glass	O	O	N.A.	O	O
4 AM Radio	O	O	STD	O	O
AM/FM Mono Radio	O	O	O	O	O
AM/FM Multiplex radio (2)	O	O	STD	O	O
Metallic paint	O	O	N.A.	O	O
Laminated windscreen (tinted/band)	O	O	STD	N.A.	N.A.
5 GS Rallye pack (4)	O	O	O	O	O
6 Driving lights (3)	O	O	O	O	O
Bodyside protection group	O	O	STD	O	O
7 Full wheelcovers	O	O	N.A.	O	O
Radial ply tyres — YR78 steel belt	O	O	STD	N.A.	N.A.
Radial ply tyres — ZR70 steel belt	O	O	STD	N.A.	N.A.
Radial ply tyres 155 SR 13	STD	STD	N.A.	O	O

(1) Radial ply tyres are mandatory options with the sports road wheels on vans.

(2) Incorporates 2 speakers — two in rear package tray.

(3) When driving lights option fitted, front rubber overriders are also fitted for increased protection.

(4) The GS Rallye pack comprises:— Driving lamps and overriders - Sports Road wheels - Soft feel 3 spoke steering wheel - Black nylon coated front bumperettes and rear bumper - Bold bodyside stripe running the length of the vehicle at bumper bar height.

STD Standard equipment on this series.
O Optional item
N.A. Not available as an option on this series

Illustrations and information presented above were correct when this publication was approved for printing.

Above: The Australian option list for the Mark 2.

*Above: The 1975
RS1800 twin – cam.
Ford claimed that 0 –
100 km/h took only
8.3 seconds.*

*Centre: Inside the
British – built RS1800
Custom (left – hand
drive export model).*

*Below: A 1975
RS2000.*

In the UK a modified 1.3 Escort Mark 2 established a fuel economy record of 118.7 mpg (2.4 L/100 km) at Boreham circuit (Essex).

1976 1.6 L.

Above: A 1976 Australian – built van with numerous factory options.

Above: A 1976 1.6 Mexico.

Left: Inside the 1976 Mexico (an RS1800 equivalent).

Above: Mass – production 16 – valve engine are not something new. This is a road version of the BDA 16 – valve all – alloy engine, as fitted to the 1976 RS1800.

Left: A works Group 2 RS1800 with the road – going equivalent in 1976.

Below: A top speed of 111 mph (179 km/h) was claimed for the 1976 RS2000.

Above: The first Mark 2 RS2000 seen downunder. Racing driver Bob Holden gets the keys from Ford Australia's then – director of sales and marketing, Max Gransden.

Left and over the page: Other angles on the 25 UK RS2000s specially imported by Ford Australia.

Below: Inside a RS2000, this time with modifications for rally use. Note the extra gauges and space for navigation equipment on left side of the instrument panel.

*Above and left: The Escapee, an
Australian dress – up pack fitted to the
1.6 – litre Escort.*

*Below: The Escort automatic transmission,
as fitted to 1300 and 1600 models.*

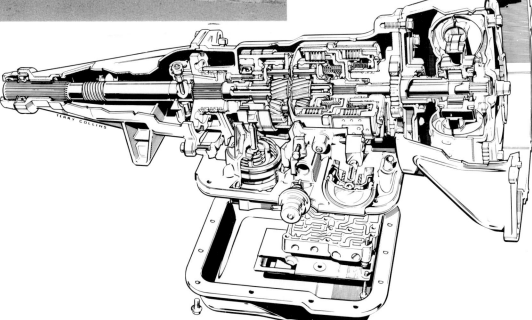

This page and opposite: The 1977 2 – litre GL two – door, the fastest Aussie – built Escort, with the 'Rally Pack' dress – up gear.

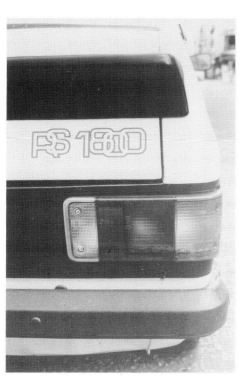

Above: Another terribly 1970s marketing special from Ford Australia: the Denim Pack Escort.

Left: RS1800 from 1978.

The British 'Series X' RS2000 (left) provided the styling inspiration for this muscular Ford Australia show car, displayed at the 1977 Sydney Motor Show.

Top and centre: The Escort Sundowner, another cash – in on the recreational vehicle boom of the late 1970s.

Left: 1979 brought a range of upgraded Escorts. The differences included an all – black grille, sports wheels and new wheel covers for the Ghia.

Right: The UK spec RS2000 Custom which replaced the Mexico.

Centre and below: The Aussie – built RS2000 was launched in 1979 in two – door and four – door versions. Automatic transmission was optional, as were the locally made Volante alloy wheels fitted to these examples. The distinctive headlight surrounds were later revived in spirit for the Laser – based TX3.

The Australian RS2000.

Left: The XR3 from 1980. By this time the Australian Escort range had given way to the Mazda – based Laser but the Escort continued to set sales records in Europe.

Left, second from top: Sadly Australian buyers were denied the Escort Cabriolet produced in Europe. This is a 1984 model.

Top right: Rallying in the days before the Escort made it downunder. This is the Roger Clark/Jim Porter Twin – Cam on its way to outright victory in the 1968 Scottish Rally.

Left: John Fitzpatrick – later to win the Bathurst 1000 in a Holden Torana – campaigning a Broadspeed 1300GT at Mallory Park in the UK in 1968.

Below: The 26,000 km London – to – Mexico World Cup Rally of 1970 saw a convincing Escort victory. This photo was taken during a reconnaissance run conducted prior to the event.

Above and left: RS1600s receive some extra body welding and last – minute checks at Ford's competition division.

Below: Ford offered a 'Clubman Pack' in the UK for the Mexico and RS1600 Escorts. It included quartz iodine lights, roll bar, bucket seats, map light, gas shocks, uprated springs and other rally equipment.

Above: A timed section at Oran Park race circuit (NSW) during the 1971 Dulux Rally. The Escort Twin – Cam is in the hands of Bob Inglis.

Below: The Bob Inglis Escort Twin – Cam on the dirt. Chris Avery was the regular navigator.

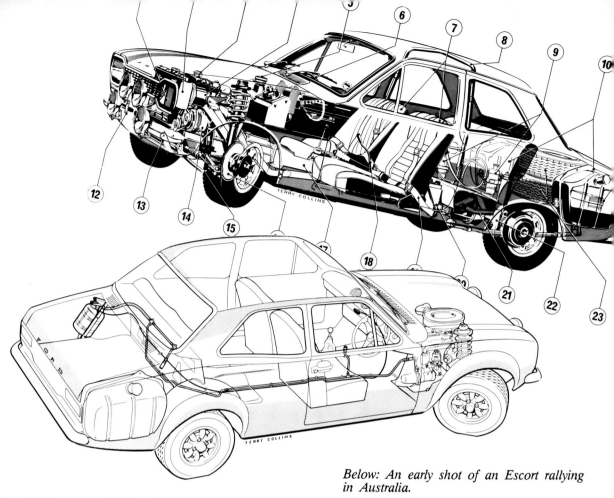

Below: An early shot of an Escort rallying in Australia.

Right: Rallycross was another success story for Escort. This shot was taken in England.

Centre: An Escort leads an HR Holden in an Australian rallycross event.

Right: An all–female Escort team competing in the Southern Cross International Rally in 1972.

Above: This Escort sports sedan built by Bill Fanning achieved remarkable results in Improved Production class in the early 1970s.

Below: A semiworks Escort at the Calder rallycross track (Victoria) in 1972.

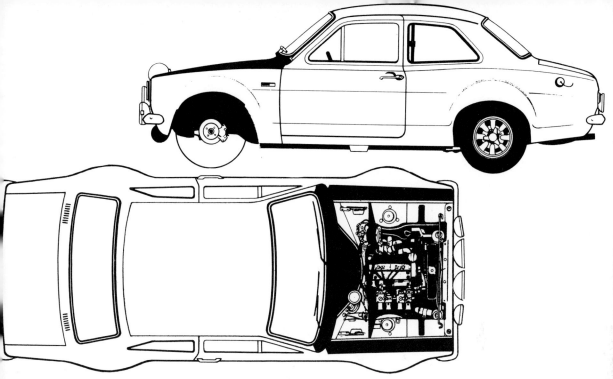

Above: A Group 2 Twin – Cam rally car.

Left and below: Escorts competing at Surfers Paradise Raceway (Qld).

Left: Works driver Ari Vatinen in a Group 2 Escort RS1800 at 9200 rpm somewhere (sideways) in Europe.

Centre: The same driver a few years later in a BDA Escort in New Zealand.

Left: Michael Stillwell — son of famous Australian race driver Bib Stillwell — at the wheel of the car which nearly won the Australian Touring Car Championship in 1972. Stillwell came second to a much larger and more powerful Camaro, narrowly missing out on performing what would have been a classic David – downs – Goliath effort.

Opposite Page: The same car later and in a bit of bother.

Above: An Escort sports sedan heading off a brace of muscular Minis.

Below: Bathurst, 1976.

Roger Clark in an RS1800 (fitted with 2 – litre BDA engine) which he campaigned in the 1976 Southern Cross International Rally. Luck did not go Ford's way.

This page and opposite: Before the 1976 Southern Cross International Rally the Escort drivers gave a demonstration of their imported machinery. The teams were Timo Makinen/Henry Liddon and Roger Clark/Jim Porter. Ford Australia backed the effort with plenty of personnel and equipment. The Escorts showed excellent form early but both ran into rear axle problems, thus helping Andrew Cowan (Mitsubishi Lancer) to win his sixth Southern Cross in eight attempts.

Inside a 1976 Southern Cross works Escort RS1800 Mark 2. Under the bonnet is the Brian Hart – prepared engine and a special strut tower brace to provide extra front – end stiffness. Also shown is Roger Clark's 1976 Southern Cross works Escort RS1800 Mark 2 engine (a 2 – litre BDA unit) about to be fitted It is shown installed over the page (top) along with another view of a Southern Cross Escort engine bay.

Southern Cross Escorts.

*An Escort Twin – Cam leading a Torana
at Surfers Paradise Raceway in 1972. The
position was reversed in the sales race.*

Above: Australian driver Greg Carr giving his all in a Mark 2 during the Southern Cross International Rally. Escorts never won the prestigious Southern Cross, although Carr won the Australian Rally Championship in an RS1800 in 1978, thwarting what would have been ten consecutive Datsun ARC victories. Carr was also a multiple winner of the Castrol International Rally.

Left: Mark 'Son of Margaret' Thatcher racing an Escort in the late 1970s. Thatcher first appeared at Bathurst (driving a Corolla) in 1979 but registered a 'Did Not Finish'.

Below: Three – times world champion Jackie Stewart tested Hannu Mikkola's works rally car at Snetterton's rallycross circuit in 1978. It was Stewart's first drive of a rally car, but he didn't hang around.

Above: Another promising Escort attack on the Southern Cross International Rally involved the pairing of Colin Bond and John Dawson – Damer. Again it failed to bear fruit.

Below: Australia's Greg Carr successfully chasing his seventh successive win in the Castrol International Rally in an RS1800 in 1980.

The much – modified Fanning Escort, perhaps the hottest Aussie racing Escort of the early 1970s.

An oversteering HQ 350 sedan is about to be overtaken by a Twin – Cam. The action occurred during a touring car support race before the Adelaide round of the 1974 Tasman series.

Opposite page: The Escort van was sold with a variety of optional dress – up packs to attract young buyers.

Above: Greg Carr again (with navigator Fred Gocentas) in the 1980 Castrol International Rally. They are descending the famous 'Mineshaft' track near Canberra with typical verve.

Opposite page: Rallying Escorts were rarely seen with all wheels on the ground, as these photos show. Escort exponent extraordinaire Roger Clark, in usual high – flying form, is about to test the sump guard.

Left: Another flying Escort, snapped during the 1000 Lakes Rally. Hannu Mikkola and Timo Makinen took first and second places.

Inside a dressed – up Escort van.

The Mark 2 body, released in Australia in 1975, gave the Escort modern European lines.

An Escort Mark 2, fitted with the Escapee dress – up pack.

Below: Ford Australia displayed this souped – up Escort at the Sydney Motor Show but the wild body kit never went on sale.

Above: In 1974 the Escort was 'yumping for joy' with 15 national and international victories to its credit, including a couple of major Aussie wins.

Below and opposite: More flying Escorts. The RS1800 (opposite bottom) in Kenya in 1977.

Left: Southern Cross International Rally, 1972.

Below and opposite: Ford's massive assault on the 1976 Southern Cross International Rally was unsuccessful despite having the services of top–ranking European drivers Roger Clark and Timo Makinen.

1972

1973

1974

1975

1976

1977

FORD ESCORT — RAC RALLY WINNER 1972-1977

Above and below: Colin Bond, has been a top–line race and rally driver for Ford and GMH. He has scored major victories – including Bathurst – for both companies. At the 1981 Sydney Motor Show a rallysprint–style 'Champion of Champions' event was held around the adjoining Showground Speedway circuit. Bond demonstrated some interesting angles.

Below (inset): Ed Mulligan practising for the rallysprint–style 'Champion of Champions' event held at the 1981 Sydney Motor Show.

Escorts appeared in the annual Bathurst enduro every year from 1970 to 1982. They scored class wins in 1972, 1976 and 1978.

ESCORT de luxe interior (above) is neatly done; GT version (below) sports extra instruments, including tacho. LEFT: Cutaway reveals Escort innards.

enter the escort

Harold Dvoretsky reports on Anglia replacement

FORD in Britain have at last replaced the venerable Anglia with a smart new car, the Escort, which looks like leading to a new battle with GM for sales in the small car field.

Cleanly styled with a modish hipline, it looks remarkably like GM's Viva/Torana models, apart from a not-so-pretty grille. Ford (Aust.) has no curent plans to market the car Down Under, as it has placed all its small-car eggs firmly in the Cortina basket—but Ford (U.K.) men seem to think it will be seen in Australia.

The Escort is a bit heavier around the window areas and presents a sturdier look than the GM counterpart but it has a prettier rear view. Where it really does steal a march on the opposition (for a short while anyway) is that it offers a choice of four engines ranging from just under 1100 cc. up to a 1600 cc. twin-cam!

One blow

Ford have done in one hit what GM are planning to do in dribs and drabs — one body, various refinements and loads of engine permutations. The market researchers say this is just what the customers are going to want — world-wide. The ideal, they say, is a smaller, roomier, comfortable handsome package with good tractability.

New Ford baby looks very like Viva in profile (top), but is less happy round grille (left). RIGHT: Note Aeroflow vents in the rear just above boot.

The Escort will appeal at one end of the scale to the pocket of the first-car buyer, while still pleasing the guy who wants to get up and go at the other. It has to be a car that's docile for mum to do the shopping. But if dad wants to drive it hard he has to be able to put more guts under the bonnet.

The result is that at one end of the Escort scale is a cross-flow, bowl-in-piston, five-bearing, four-cylinder 1098 cc. motor giving 53 bhp at 5500 rpm and returning a claimed 36 mpg. At the other end is the volatile Lotus-Ford twin-cam of 1558 cc. with hemi-head, 115 bhp at 6000 rpm and 115 mph. Fuel injection, mag wheels, limited slip diffs, etc., are available for the rally man.

In between the de luxe 1100 (there is a price-matching "basic" car selling alongside the standard Viva) and the twin-cam are the "super" with 1298 cc., 63 bhp, and the Escort GT with the same basic donk, a twin-choke Weber, high-compression head and high-lift camshaft giving 75 bhp.

The Escort Deluxe will, at £517 stg. basic, be £13 lower in price when it leaves the factory than the equivalent Viva. It might not sound much, but when the stops are out, and tax has been levied, the salesman with £20 stg. to play with must have an edge over the opposition.

The space-race

Internally the Escort offers a very neat package with oodles of room for the driver. The furnishings look good and the dashboard is neat, tidy and attractive. There's the now-usual aeroflow ventilation and heaters as standard.

Rear-seat legroom is no better, no worse than others when the front seat is right back on the slide (the front, tip-up seats have a built-in locking device to prevent the back passenger pushing them — and their occupants — up, in a head-on crash).

Speaking of safety, the Escort seems to match up to the American regs with all the necessary new ideas — anti-burst locks, thick padded facia panel and (hooray) an ignition key lock located on the side of the steering column where the kneecap is unlikely to whack it. Most of the controls are of flexible material and a foot-operated rubber button to the left of the clutch pedal controls the four-nozzle windscreen washers. The steering wheel is deeply dished for safety with a single stalk mounted on the column to control the headlamp flasher, dipper, direction indicators and horn.

There's a big boot with almost 10 cu. ft. of usable space — almost double that of the Anglia.

Ford are still being damn mean about the size of their fuel tanks. A capacity of only nine gallons isn't really enough for the higher-powered models —even a gallon extra would help.

Like GM, Ford make front disc brakes an optional extra for the two lower-priced versions though the GT and twin-

(This article continued on page 84)

Cosworth engine turns Ford's smallest into a real rubber-layer, reports Karl Ludvigsen

FORD of Britain has to be one of the most adventurous and irrepressible automakers in the world. They dominate Formula 3 with their engines now as they did Formula Junior before. Then they backed Keith Duckworth and took over Formulas 2 and 1 to boot. They had the nerve to make up a racing formula in their own name and dared to allow it to become the huge success it is today. They compete successfully in the great rallies with the most ordinary looking sedans. And now, with a 16-valve Cosworth engine in an Escort, they're about to turn loose on the highways a humble-looking sedan that's an absolute rocket. It's nothing more or less than a light economy car powered by half a Grand Prix Cosworth-Ford V8.

In January, 1968 the Escort was unveiled, as a new bottom-of-the-line model for Ford of Britain and later for Ford of Germany as well (Australia too — see page 55). In January, 1969

TOP: Discreet badges and wide wheels are only signs that there is more to this car than meets the eye.
ABOVE: Wedge-shaped combustion chambers, showing valve faces. Flat-top pistons are utilised.
LEFT: Other side of head shows valve springs, big side-draught carburettors.

FORD'S MINI-BOMB

BDA engine installed. Big air cleaner helps keep deep-breathing Weber carburettors quiet. In road-going tune BDA produces 120 bhp, but FVA version puts out up to 250 bhp!

The Cosworth-Ford BDA engine was first shown in one of the new Capris. Ford calls it the final phase of the joint program with Cosworth Engineering that produced the all-conquering Formula 1 and 2 engines. Now, as of January, 1970, it's certain that the controversial BDA will reach production.

With this typical directness, Keith Duckworth of Cosworth calls his new engine the "BDA" because it has Belt Drive to its twin overhead camshafts. Otherwise, in the spacing of its four valves per cylinder and the 40-degree included angle between them, it's an almost exact tracing of the FVA Formula 2 engine. Both use a Ford 1599 cc cylinder block. While the FVA has a larger bore and shorter stroke, the BDA keeps the stock crankshaft, connecting rods, bottom-end bearings and dimensions of 81.0 x 77.6 mm.

A piston that's virtually flat-topped replaces the heavier stock bowl-in-piston part. Matched with a shallow fully-machined combustion chamber with room for a single central 14mm spark plug, it gives a 10 to one compression ratio. This is high, yet the engine is happy on fuel of only 92 octane, with an ignition advance that's zero at rest and 24 degrees at 6000

rpm. Ignition is stock, with the addition of a rev-limiter, and carburetion is by twin side-draft 40 mm Webers as it was on the Cortina-Lotus twin-cam engine that this one will replace.

So it could be easily machined inside and out, Duckworth made the new aluminium cylinder head in two levels. The top one carries the camshaft bearings and the small cup-type tappets. Unscrew it at 12 points, take it off, and you expose the coil valve springs, one per valve, and the adjusting shims. Because the valves are so small (1.22 and 1.00 inches) and light and the valve lift so low (0.35 inch) only one spring is needed to keep the valves following the cams up to 8250 rpm.

That's faster than the stock bottom-end parts will let the engine turn safely. Its peak power of 120 bhp (net) is reached at 6000 rpm. It

actually climbs a little further to 122 bhp at 6500, and the BDA winds to 7000 with no effort at all. Just by removing the air cleaner the output can be made to jump to 129 bhp. Maximum torque is 110 lb ft at 4000 rpm. Early engines had a sharp jump in output at 3000 rpm after a flat spot at 2500 but BDA no. 13, which I drove for several hundred miles, was smooth as could be all the way up the scale.

Removing the air cleaner isn't such a bad idea; in fact it's inevitable if you want to get at the back two spark plugs. Somewhere there will have to be an oil dipstick but on this "Coscort" it was literally out of sight. Special installation features include a torque strut from the back of the engine to the firewall and an oil cooler at the front left of the radiator piped in and out through the oil filter carrier. A black fibreglass guard covers the ¾-inch cogged belt that drives the camshafts and the jackshaft for the distributor (hidden under the Webers) and the oil and fuel pumps.

Weighing only 280lb, the BDA is a perfect fit under the hood of the 1730lb Escort Twin Cam. It doesn't look like much, if the truth be told, but looks have never been more deceiving. This is one of the most able all-round small engines ever installed in an automobile. With small tappet clearances, from 5 to 7 thousandths, there's no noise at all from the valve gear. The belt's quiet too. At the smooth 600 rpm idle the BDA is measurably quieter than most small pushrod engines.

With this amazingly cultivated engine it was fun to pick up a friend in this plain-looking white Escort with the wide-rimmed wheels and drive quietly around a few corners — then stand on it hard in second gear. The quiet exhaust changes instantly to a low, menacing sound, for all the world like the staccato boom of the unblown Offy filtered through a muffler. It's a rich, mellow, satisfying sound, marred only by a resonant rasp as the engine spins through the 6300 rpm range. Above 6500 the "boy-racer" racket disappears again. Meanwhile the Escort has been rocketing forward, its passenger stunned by the speed with which it eats up its environment.

This British equivalent of the Z-28 Camaro is a joy to race up and down through its precise quick four-speed box. At every opportunity I put my foot flat down to experience that insistent moan, that stimulating slug in the shoulder blades and the thrill of winding that solid little BDA out, out, out to the 7500 rpm at which the Ford people tell me it's safe. At 7000 it does 40 in first, 59 in second and 84 mph in third gear. With the 3.77 axle it has no trouble reaching 117 in top gear.

When I picked up the Escort at Ford's London garage I was cautioned by Alf Belson, "Be sure to rev her up in traffic now and then." In spite of driving it all-out like a sports car I did run into some misfiring trouble which defied analysis. I concur with the Ford opinion that it was probably an atypical random electrical glitch. "She's a thirsty little beast," Belson also warned me. But I was happy with the mileage of almost 19 miles per U.S. gallon I measured on one run.

For a basically cheap car (without BDA) the Escort was pleasant to live in. Its simple, neat dash carried a battery voltage gauge as well as the tach and dials for oil pressure and water temperature. You have to adapt to the driving position, with the small steering wheel offset one way, the seat slightly angled another way. It feels arbitrary but it works.

Least pleasing are the "Coscort's" riding qualities. It handles small bumps well enough but on big ones it seems to pitch and bound with enough energy to go into orbit. When you see a bump coming you just duck your head and grip the wheel. This ride is a normal Escort feature and wasn't expected to be any different on the Twin Cam BDA, with its front anti-roll bar, rear radius rods and ¾-inch lowering blocks at the rear leaf springs.

Ride is one thing and road grip is another. Rolling on India Super Autoband Radial tyres, 165SR x 13, this Escort had handling to match its performance. I didn't measure its lateral acceleration but judging by the vertiginous feeling it generates around constant-radius turns it has to be very high by road standards, say a usable 0.85 or 0.9g. You have to haul the understeering nose back in but the Escort doesn't drift out. It sticks and keeps on sticking, feeling like a car developed mainly for circuit racing, not rallying. With 3½ turns lock to lock the steering is sensitive and responsive.

When I tried the BDA Ford was still trying to figure out what to do with it. They don't need it for racing, where the old Lotus-developed Twin Cam is still doing a good job. But for international rallying — as the latest Monte showed — they need more power to be able to compete for outright wins. The power is there. Tests show that with the belt drive the BDA can be made to produce up to 180 bhp. Switching to a gear drive to the cams lets it go to 9000 rpm and an output of 230 bhp — still from 97.5 cubic inches.

Ford Advanced Vehicle Operations, set up with manufacturing facilities in Germany and assembly area in Britain, was recently formed to add a little performance spice to Ford's everyday product pudding. Its role in Europe will be analagous to the one Kar Kraft plays in the U.S. today, with its Brighton plant producing special Ford models like the Talladega and the Boss 429 Mustangs. An Escort with the Cosworth BDA engine is AVO's first project, due to be marketed in Europe through selected dealers in April.

There may be some changes in the BDA as conceived by Duckworth. Ford engineers are less than in love with the double-decker head construction, which even skilled mechanics have trouble putting together in a reasonable length of time. They've worked out a casting design that will permit making it in one piece. It would be a more complicated casting but would make the engine easier and cheaper to maintain in the field.

Without taxes the eight-valve Escort Twin Cam costs $2300 in Britain. We can't guess yet what the extra eight

valves will add to the price but it can't be too much. In fact the "Cosworth", is likely to be one of the best performance buys in the automotive world. It packs more sheer exhilaration into a small, simple package than anything I've driven in a long, long time.

Ford BDA-Escort acceleration:

0-30 mph	3.2 sec.
0-40	4.5
0-50	6.2
0-60	8.3
0-70	10.6
0-80	13.2

ESCORT

(Continued from page 81)

cam have them as standard. The 8-in. drum brakes seem adequate enough and with a total lining area for the 1100 of 75.4 sq. in., and 81.7 for the 1300 sedan they should stop both cars under most conditions.

Steering is rack and pinion and the turning circle of only 29 ft. most acceptable.

Chassis, brakes

Underneath, Ford have stuck to the old and known. Up front there's the usual McPherson layout with coils, telescopic hydraulic double-acting shock absorbers integral with the wheel spindle and located in the body in a rubber-mounted upper bearing. A new feature is the lower wheel location by a track control arm and a rubber-bushed compression strut which is mounted on the body side member. The idea is for the suspension unit to absorb both vertical and fore-and-aft road shocks.

At the rear the 47 in. asymmetrical semi-elliptic leaves have double-acting hydraulic shock absorbers mounted at an angle of 60 deg. to the rear axle.

Now this doesn't sound a bad layout but I would have liked to see a bit more location on the 1100 and 1300 standard cars. On the GT version there are twin radius arms while the twin-cam gets the treatment all the Escorts should have: two trailing links and a Panhard rod to really locate the axle.

The 1100, 1300 and 1300 GT versions have 12 in. wheels. Cross-ply tyres are standard on the 1100 and 1300 while the GT gets radials as standard equipment. The twin-cam has 13 in. 5.5 J rims and radials as standard.

Sound like a good package? I'll say. And what are the chances of it being released in Australia?

While there might be doubt in the minds of some Down Under that the new Escort will be seen in Australia, there doesn't seem to be any doubt in the minds of Ford's U.K. boys that it certainly will.

It might mean the end of the lower-powered 1300 Cortina in Australia.

(Continued on page 88)

TOP: Shape is already familiar through overseas publicity. Australian car doesn't vary. LEFT: Interior of Super 1300 version.

ECONO-ESCORT

Ford muscles into the small car field with the low-priced, practical and attractive Escort reports Barry Cooke

FORD plugged another hole in its range on March 20, when it released the low-priced and long-awaited Escort.

Mr. Bill Bourke, Ford's MD had some pretty ambitious things to say about the car — among them that it is going to knock the small Jap cars off the pedestal they've occupied for some time.

He also forecast doom for GM-H as Australia's No. 1 car maker, predicting that Ford would be top dog by the end of the decade.

Mr. Bourke's confidence in the future of Ford is not ill-founded, because the company does have — we think — the best **range** of vehicles of the local manufacturers, and the Escort strengthens that aspect of their operation even further.

The car is initially offered in three forms — the base model which sells for $1770, the Super which sells for $1920, and the GT which is marked at $2350.

The standard and Super use an 1100 cc engine with a 1300 as a $90 option. Bowl-in-piston, cross flow types, they develop 53 and 61.5 bhp respectively.

The GT uses the 1300 motor uprated to 76 bhp. Not yet released, but slated to appear about May is a Lotus twin-cam-powered Escort, which will sell for the astonishing price of $3000.

The demand for this car will be mammoth, so get your order in now.

The Escort in all its other forms — we haven't driven a twin cam yet — feels pretty much like the other small Fords — Cortina and Capri — lively, responsive, and a little fragile.

They have the strange habit of wandering slightly at high speed, and are inclined to wag their ass-ends on rough going.

The ride on poor surfaces is distinctly bouncy, and steering behaviour is noticeable understeer at low speeds, inclining to better balance as speed rises.

Instrumentation is basic in all but the GT, and interior trim features a lot of plastic and rubber — but the Escort hasn't got this on its own.

Judging on appearances alone, the Escort looks to be under-wheeled and under-tyred. We didn't measure performance, but will run a test in the next issue.

The cars come in Ford's usual range of imaginative colors, but don't look so good in this way-out garb as do the more shapely Capris.

This won't stop them selling — particularly to the young folk at whom the car is directed.

Ford place great emphasis on the "youth market" in which they lump everyone under 30, and there's not the slightest doubt in my mind that many Escorts will end up in the hands of these people.

Just how GM-H, BLMC, Toyota and Datsun will answer the Escort threat remains to be seen.

One thing is certain. Things are really hotting up in the small car field. ●

PROFILE shot emphasises the clean simplicity of Escort styling. Ford Motor Co. claims that the shape is an extremely aerodynamic one.

Ford reckons it will take the small car market by storm with their latest bouncy baby, the Escort. Here's our report on how two of them stack up

IN many ways the parent of the child is reflected in Ford's newest baby, the Escort.

It is a bouncy, brash little motor car — and it is marketed by a bouncy — and sometimes brash — company.

More and more in recent years, Ford has switched its marketing attack to the younger generation. This trend has reached its peak with the Escort, which is being promoted by a series of advertisements and TV commercials that can only be described as op, pop, and just plain way-out.

Ford call the Escort "the going thing", and they've just recently launched a pop group called appropriately the "Going Thing".

That is indication enough of their deep commitment to the younger generation of buyers.

If they're aiming to get youngsters into the Escort, we can only report that they are going about it in exactly the right way.

The various Escorts we've driven in recent weeks have all had a feeling of response and liveliness that will certainly be attractive to kids.

And if the car feels right, it also looks right too. Or at least, those with the various eye-catching options do.

Superoo decals, ape-tape, and flashy wheel trims may not count for much with the oldies, but the kids love it.

Add to this argument a very reasonable price structure, and you have a recipe for sales success.

Ford Escorts start at $1770 — but that's a "cheapie" no-one but fleet owners would buy.

The car most kids will buy is the Escort Super — at $1920 — which makes it considerably cheaper than the four-cylinder Torana, and reasonably competitive with the comparably-equipped Japanese.

The Super we subjected to test recently was fitted with an optional ($90) 1300 cc motor, which, at 61.5

bhp is 8.5 bhp stronger than the standard 1100 cc motor.

The other subject of this twin test is the GT Escort, which uses a Weber-aspirated 1300 motor developing 75 bhp.

The GT, which has better instrumentation as well as the "breathed-on" motor, different gearbox final drive ratios, and wider wheels, sells for $2350.

Mechanicals

All Escort engines are of the cross-flow type introduced about three years ago on the Cortina. The 1300 is identical with the Cortina, but the 1100 is an exclusive Escort development.

The 1100 measures 80.98 mm by 53.29 mm, has a capacity of 1098 cc and develops 53 bhp.

The 1300 measures 80.98 across the bore, has a stroke of 62.99, and a capacity of 1298. These engines use Ford-made downdraught carburettors. The GT uses a Weber double-choke downdraught, has a high lift camshaft, and four branch exhaust.

The standard transmission is a four-speed manual on the 1100 and 1300, with optional three-speed

INTERIOR of Super (left) is almost identical with interior of GT (right) except for the latter's additional instrumentation. Padded, leather bound steering wheels are extra cost option on both cars, but carpets and good quality upholstery are standard equipment.

automatic. The GT is available only in four-speed manual form.

The gearbox and final drive ratios on the GT are different from the others.

Both use direct top gear ratios, the GT giving 16.2 mph/1000 rpm, the 1300 15.8.

Although overall gearing is different, there isn't much practical difference in terms of speed in gears. The Super has ratios of 3.66, 2.19, 1.43 and 1.00 with a differential of 3.90. These give maximums of 28, 48, 68, and 85.

The GT uses ratios of 3.34, 2.00, 1.42, and 1.00 with a "shorter" 4.125 final drive. It has maximums in the gears of 30, 50, 70, and 95. Despite the variation, the gearing isn't really any closer — which strikes us as being an exercise in futility.

Of course, the GT's comparative low-speed inefficiency may have had something to do with the selection of ratios. It produces 74.5 lb. ft. at 4300 rpm, while the 1300 produces 75.5 at 2500. One more lb. ft. at 1800 revs less!

From these figures you might gather that the 1300 is a nicer car to drive around the city where high speed performance isn't so important. If you did you'd be dead right.

The 1300 is much more flexible and trickles around with surprisingly little gear shifting — if the throttle is manipulated with sympathy.

In fact, there is not much difference in straight line performance between the two until 50 mph is reached. The GT gets there in 9 sec., the 1300 takes 10.5. Sixty comes up in 12.8 for the GT, 15.5 for the 1300.

Performance-wise, the benefits of the GT configuration are not felt until one is confronted with a stretch of winding sporty-type road where power and torque at high revs are useful.

Suspension is virtually identical, although the GT has ½ in. wider wheels. At the front MacPherson strut layout is used, while at the rear semi elliptics are fitted, and in the case of the GT, twin radius arms as well.

Both cars are inclined to lack

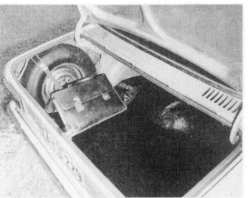

ABOVE: GT Escort corners at speed. Car gives impression that roll is excessive but this is belied in pic.
LEFT: Boot is generous.
BELOW LEFT: GT motor, showing exhausts.
BELOW RIGHT: 1300 cc. standard gives 61 bhp.

ESCORT

directional stability under certain circumstances, there being subtle changes in attitude under power-on and power-off situations.

But a series of potholes in bitumen or a particularly rough corner on an unmade road, is just as likely to point both cars towards the shrubbery.

When this happens, the sharp rack and pinion steering comes in very handy.

Ride is pretty bouncy on poor surfaces, and the seat belts need to be cinched up tight to make sure head and roof don't make contact.

The Escort is — particularly non-GT varieties — an exceedingly quiet car; undoubtedly the quietest small car we've ever driven. Some of the Japanese manufacturers would do well to take a leaf out of the Ford keep-it-quiet book.

Not only are mechanical sounds damped, but also road noise. That's a very notable achievement in a car so small and Ford are to be complimented on it — because noise can be a very tiring element on long-distance trips.

Handling is predictable enough low-speed understeer which balances out as the speed of the car rises.

Our test cars were shod with optional radial tyres, which improved adhesion greatly. We weren't able to break the tail of either easily on dry bitumen, but when they finally did come unstuck, it was all very predictable and free from drama.

Front disc brakes are standard on all 1300 cc Escorts, and these worked well. We recorded best stops of .92 g with both cars, which was surprising because each had different brand radials, and we had expected at least a slight variation.

There was a tendency with both to lock up at the rear when the brakes grew hot from repeated use. Neither car is particularly thirsty. On short trips to rural areas beyond the city fringes where 70 mph cruising is attainable, the GT returned 31 and the 1300 34.

We figure these are pretty close to what private owners will get.

Interior

Apart from extra instrumentation the 1300 Super and GT are identical internally. The GT sports a full set of instruments in a neat arrangement right in front of the driver. Unfortunately, not all of them are visible all the time — or even part of the time — thanks to the wheel rim and driver's right hand. The selection includes speedo and tacho, water temperature and fuel gauges, ammeter and oil pressure gauges.

The Super has speedo, water temperature and fuel gauges, and

warning lights for oil pressure and amps. The GT has two-speed wipers.

Both test cars were fitted with optional GS packs, which include side-stripes, wheel trims and padded, leather-bound steering wheels. This is the sort of "gingerbread" that will make the car attractive to youngsters.

Front seats are fairly comfortable buckets with an articulated backrest that tilts to allow access to the rear bench.

Rear legroom is minimal, and juggling the front seats on their runners doesn't help adults much, although children have sufficient space.

Rearward adjustment of the driver's seat is somewhat limited, and long-legged six-footers might have trouble with their knees and elbows.

Upholstery is a textured vinyl, and carpets cover the floors.

The Escort, like other English Fords uses the Aeroflow flow-through ventilation system.

The fresh air outlets are located atop the dash and in the centre, so that they're a little too removed from occupants to give an impression of fresh air flowing freely into the cabin. We prefer the Cortina/Capri arrangement with the vents located at either end of the dash — although people living in cold climates might not agree.

Boot space is very generous for so small a car — easily capable of taking the duffel of four adults.

The spare is located upright and on the left of the boot — where it doesn't interfere with luggage, or present an inconvenience in the case of unloading for a flat tyre.

We've commented previously on English Ford products being generally rattly and fragile-feeling. While the Escort feels more robust on rough surfaces than either the Cortina or Capri, it still has quite a few rattles, emanating mostly it seems, from the region of the rear suspension.

Obviously people who buy an Escort should also invest in a spanner, because both test cars gave the impression that it might be needed from time to time.

Despite its failings, and there aren't many, the Escort is very much a car for the '70s and it will find wide acceptance among the people of the '70s. ●

(This article continued from page 84)

Pricewise it would be about the same. The Cortina is ckd ex-U.K. — the Escort could be the same.

I can't see Ford letting GM get too much of a head start with the Torana down there.

On the road — in Morocco

Almost 1000 miles through Morocco from the warm winter plains up to the snow-lined Atlas Mountains in three of the four new models showed they live up to their specifications. With few reservations they're obviously going to be a great sales success.

The seating is excellent and the driving position leaves little to be desired.

The rack and pinion steering is light and precise and the 29-ft. turning circle is outstanding.

Dashboard layout throughout the range is excellent — only in the GT where four smaller gauges (for fuel, battery voltage, temperature and oil pressure) are mounted does the steering wheel rim obscure the driver's vision of them.

The new gearbox has a short movement but for the long, fast stretches and the Moroccan-type road I would prefer a taller third gear. As it was, 59 mph for the 1100 and around 64 mph for the 1300 models didn't seem quite enough.

The clutch pedal pressure, cable operated, must be the lightest in the business. The drum brakes on the 1100 and 1300 seem adequate, though under extreme braking from higher speeds there was some tramp from the live rear axle. This could have been caused because at the last minute Ford engineers decided to remove the two tramp bars from all but the 1600 twin-cam version.

Ford say they did this because the bars were transmitting noise from the axle to the car. I hope they put them back, and be damned to the noise. On the slightly stiffer sprung and front disc-braked GT version of the 1300 they are definitely needed.

Under heavy braking the 1300 GT locks its rear brakes, but the tramp noticeable on three versions of 1100 and 1300 standard models I drove didn't eventuate. The 1100 and 1300 versions rode flat and softly around fast corners, the stiffer GT was a real rumbler giving a rather notchy and none-too-pleasant ride on some indifferent road surfaces. All the cars were on Pirelli Cinturato radials (optional extras on the 1100 and 1300 and standard on the GT).

Top speeds seemed genuine enough. Corrected speedo readings gave 81 mph for the 1100 (the second version I drove had a speedo 1 mph slow throughout the range). The 1300 was only a little better at 82 mph (indicated 89 mph) and 90 mph (indicated 97) on the GT. The first 1100 had a fantastic vibration at around 75 mph which disappeared as though by magic at 78 mph. Fuel consumptions for our flat-out running turned out at only 24 mpg for the 1100 and 1300, and 26 mpg for the GT.

The 1100 got to 50 mph in 14 sec., to 60 in 21 sec., while the 1300 got to 50 mph in 11.7 sec. and to 60 mph in 16.9 sec.

The GT got to 50 mph in 9.6 sec., to 60 in 13.2 sec., to 70 in 19.1 sec., and to 80 mph in 28.2 sec.

Only one twin-cam found its way to Morocco and time didn't allow more than a shuffle around the car park. In any case it would seem to be a car one would appreciate better on a long Continental run, which I hope to do in the near future. ●

DATA SHEET— ESCORT GT & SUPER

Where variations occur GT figures appear in brackets.

Manufacturer: Ford Motor Co. of Aust.
Test cars supplied by them.
Price as tested: $2130 ($2470).

ENGINE

Water cooled, 4 cylinders in line. Cast iron block, five main bearings.
Bore x stroke .... 80.98 x 62.99 mm
Capacity .... 1298 cc
Compression .... 9.0 to 1 (9.2 to 1)
Carburettor .... Ford d'draught (Weber 2-choke d'draught)
Fuel pump .... mechanical
Fuel tank .... 9 gallons
Fuel recommended .... super
Valve gear .... p'rod ohv
Max. power (gross) .... 61.5 bhp at 5000 rpm (75 at 6000)
Max. torque ....75.5 lb.ft. at 2500 rpm (74.5 at 4300)
Electrical system .... 12v, 40 amp hr battery.

TRANSMISSION

Four speed manual all synchro gearbox, single dry plate clutch.

Gear	Ratio	Mph/1000 Rpm	Max mph
Rev.	4.24 (4.25)	—	—
1st	3.66 (3.34)	—	28 (30)
2nd	2.19 (2.00)	—	48 (50)
3rd	1.43 (1.42)	—	68 (70)
4th	1.00	15.8 (16.2)	85 (95)
Final drive ratio			3.90 to 1 (4.125)

CHASSIS

Wheelbase .... 7ft. 10½in.
Track front .... 4ft. 1in.
Track rear .... 4ft. 2in.
Length .... 13ft.
Width .... 5ft. 1¾in.
Height .... 4ft. 5in.
Clearance .... 6¼in.
Kerb weight .... 16 cwt.
Weight distribution front/rear ....53/47 percent
lb/bhp ....29.1 lb (23.7)

SUSPENSION

Front: Independent by MacPherson struts, wishbones, and anti-roll bar, telescopic dampers
Rear: Live axle with semi-elliptic leaf springs, telescopic dampers (GT — twin radius arms too).
Brakes: 8.6 in. disc/drum, servo assisted. 218 sq. in. of swept area.
Steering .... Rack and pinion
Turns lock to lock 3.5
Turning circle .... 29ft.
Wheels: Steel disc with 155 by 12 tubeless radial ply tyres.

PERFORMANCE

Top speed .... 85 mph (95)
Average (both ways) ....84.2 mph (93.6)
Standing quarter mile .... 19.9 sec. (18.5)

Acceleration

Zero to	seconds
30 mph	4.7 (3.7)
40 mph	7.4 (5.9)
50 mph	10.5 (9.0)
60 mph	15.5 (12.9)
70 mph	23.0 (18.6)
80 mph	37.1 (27.4)

	3rd	top
20-40 mph	5.5 (6.2)	— —
30-50	5.7 (5.1)	8.0 (8.3)
40-60	6.8 (5.6)	9.5 (9.0)
50-70	— (6.8)	11.2 (10.0)

BRAKING: Five crash stops from 60 mph.

Stop	percent G	pedal pressure
1	.90 (.88)	56 lb. (58)
2	.92 (.91)	58 lb. (58)
3	.90 (.92)	58 lb. (61)
4	.88 (.90)	57 lb. (59)
5	.86 (.87)	59 lb. (61)

Consumption: 34 mpg over 386 miles including all tests; (31 mpg over 314 miles including all tests).

Speedo error

Indicated mph	30	40	50	60	70
Actual mph	28	37	46	56	65
	(32)	(40)	(50)	(60)	(68)

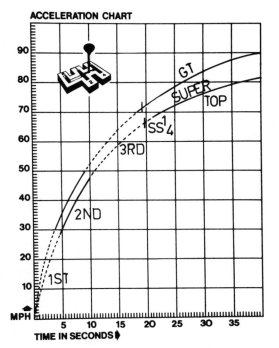

ACCELERATION CHART

TIME IN SECONDS

HOW ESCORT COMPARES

MAXIMUM SPEED (mean) M.P.H.
Ford Escort Super ($2130)
Ford Escort GT ($2470)
Toyota Corolla 1200 ($1849)

0-60 M.P.H. SECONDS
Ford Escort Super ($2130)
Ford Escort GT ($2470)
Toyota Corolla 1200 ($1849)

M.P.G. Overall
Ford Escort Super ($2130)
Ford Escort GT ($2470)
Toyota Corolla 1200 ($1849)

STANDING START ¼ MILE (secs)
Ford Escort Super
Ford Escort GT
Toyota Corolla 1200

ESCORT TWIN CAM

MODERN MOTOR road TEST

Another Bathurst machine, the Escort Twin Cam has all it takes to make it on the mountain, but not enough to make it on the road.

SUPERFICIALLY, there's not much difference between the Escort twin cam and the Escort 1300 GT. Despite this, even a cursory glance immediately suggests that the TC is a different motor car. The knock kneed stance of the front wheels (which have about 1½ deg. of negative camber) and the wide-based wheels (they're 5.5 in. as against the GT's 4.5) are giveaway clues for the really keen car watcher.

Refreshingly, the Escort TC we've just finished testing was almost completely free of the garish ornamentation Ford is inclined to heap upon its "supercars".

No blacking on the bonnet, not gold stripes or hood pins. Just a "Superoo" decal and a restrained flank badge that says "Twin cam" against a background of green and black and white chequer.

From an appointments point of view, the TC doesn't vary from the 1300 GT we tested in the June 1970 issue of Modern Motor.

It has the same comprehensive display of instruments although the calibrations have been modified to suit the TC's uprated performance. The speedo reads to 140 mph, and the tacho goes to 8000, with a redline at 6500 rpm.

The other gauges, which are neatly arranged in four-square echelon to the right of the main dials include oil pressure, ammeter, fuel contents (hopelessly inaccurate incidentally) and engine temperature gauges.

Major controls are black piano-key type switches for lights wipers, and fan blower, a pull-out choke, and a steering column wand for the directionals and main beam selector.

The steering wheel is a terrific little leather-padded job, that really contributes tremendously to the TC's roadability.

Otherwise the TC looks just like the GT. The floors are carpeted, the front seats are individuals with non-reclining backrests (they tilt to allow access to the rear bench), covered in a combination of textured and leather grain vinyl. Reasonable comfort is all they afford.

Whether done to save cost or improve engine cooling we don't know, but the front of the TC is distinguished from its lesser brothers by having "bumperettes" rather than a full width bumper.

Together with those slanty wheels they add considerably to the aggressive frontal appearance of the car.

Mechanics

Mechanically, of course the differences are enormous. The big part of the difference lies in the engine, which is an alloy-and-iron four-cyl. twin cam built by Lotus. Of 1558 cc. it is the same unit that powers Elans, and Elan Plus 2's.

It runs in comparatively unstressed form, but still, with the aid of two double-choke side-draught Weber carburettors — 40 DCOE's — it produces 115 bhp at 6000 rpm and 106

ESCORT TWIN CAM

lb. ft. of torque at 4500 rpm.

Compression ratio is 9.5 to 1, and cylinder dimensions are oversquare at 82.5 by 72.9 mm.

Maximum engine revs are 6600 rpm and to make sure you observe this limit Lotus fit a cut-out device to their distributor which automatically inhibits the engine from exceeding 6600.

It is of course, possible to remove this cut out and this is done to all racing TC's.

The engine uses an iron block, alloy cylinder head and five main bearings for the crankshaft. The overhead camshafts actuate slanted valves and specific output is 73.8 bhp/litre.

The motor, which carries the name "Lotus" atop the timing case cover is coupled to a close-ratio four-speed all-synchromesh gearbox which allows maximum of 39, 58, 84 and 115 mph.

In use, the gearshift is really brilliant, slipping through the gate like the proverbial hot knife. Short throws and a strong synchromesh make really fast changes a breeze.

Suspension is beefed up ordinary Escort.

The front is MacPherson strut with the coils that this name naturally implies, while springing at the back is by semi-elliptic leaves.

Disc brakes of 9¼ in. diameter are fitted at the front with drums at the rear. A servo assist is fitted and total swept area is 190 sq. in.

On the road

The TC is a willing enough starter hot or cold, although after overnight inactivity in Sydney's winter a touch of choke was necessary — and there was still a pronounced reluctance to idle.

Once warm, the engine ticks over — none too smoothly — at about 700 rpm. Throttle response is not brilliant until the revs wind up, the engine being decidedly sluggish below 2000 rpm, and not really "getting with it" until 4000 is reached.

Below 4000, the car will rumble along happily enough, but less peaky performers like Corollas and so on will almost invariably show the TC a clean pair of heels for the first 50 yards.

Once the tacho needle touches 4000, the effect is almost galvanic. The exhaust note gets hard, the car squats down visibly under the effects of the power getting to the road, and the TC owner is on his way.

Driven with enterprise, it is possible to keep the TC in the powerband between 4000 and 6000 rpm, but the car is in these conditions rather noisy — although the low frequency vibrations that fill the cabin when the engine is just idling along, disappear.

The vibrations and rattles are something we've complained about in other Escorts and the TC is no different. In fact, it's worse if anything, thanks to the lumpiness of the engine low down and the firmness of the beefed-up suspension.

These things combine to make the TC a not-very-pleasant around-town car.

On the open road the situation improves dramatically. As we've already pointed out the character of the TC changes once the magic 4000 rpm mark is reached.

A similar metamorphosis takes place when the driver points it up a winding bitumen road.

We've not driven a road car with such neutral steering characteristics before. Just turn the little steering wheel and the TC responds accordingly. It is tremendous fun while the road surface stays smooth.

Once the bitumen breaks up, the ride becomes harsh and the car won't point so immaculately.

On rough, gravelly roads the situation is considerably worse.

Over our 12-mile rally-type section, which is admittedly quite rough, the TC often gave the impression that it was airborne and seldom pointed in precisely the direction we wanted.

With that hard suspension it wasn't long before things started coming unstuck in the cabin. First the radio lost one of the screws holding it to the dash and drooped. Then a section of the underdash moulding came adrift.

Fortunately, we got back onto good bitumen before any irreparable damage was done

But this sort of thing would put a sour taste in the mouth of any owner, no matter how understanding he might be.

The car corners with virtually no lean, and only once on dry bitumen were we able to break the tail loose; a combination of high speed and the engine "getting on the cam" at the crucial moment hung the tail out momentarily.

But it was all very controllable and the car responded like lightning to steering correction.

The brakes are most adequate for normal use but we imagine any private owner contemplating use of the car in rallies and short circuit club racing might be advised to fit harder linings all round.

As it is, the car stops rapidly and controllably with little dive and great stability. We did feel that there was some lag between pedal movement and actual brake application, but it could have been a characteristic of the individual car.

Around town, we found the TC surprisingly economical, returning a figure of between 26 and 27 mpg. Considering the robust performance offered by the engine, that's most acceptable. Hard driven by the enterprising driver, this figure would almost certainly drop; but we see no reason why the average private owner wouldn't get 26 mpg.

The car was a disappointment to us in that it isn't particularly happy when used as a commuter. We had expected it to be more tractable around town.

And we do wish Ford would pay a little more attention to the detail finish of their English models. If the TC was as well finished as a Falcon we'd have no cause for complaint.

In its present form however, we can see it acquitting itself well at Mt. Panorama and providing handling and performance-conscious drivers with many miles of sheer driving enjoyment.

But as Road and Track tunesmith Fred Gibson said, "It's not a car for the ordinary fred." He should know ●

DATA SHEET—
FORD ESCORT TWIN CAM

Manufacturer: Ford Motor Co. of Aust.,
Homebush, N.S.W.
Test car supplied by them.
Price as tested: $3,000

ENGINE
Water cooled, 4 cylinders in line. Cast iron block, five main bearings.
Bore x stroke: .... 82.5 x 72.9 mm
Capacity .... 1558 cc
Compression .... 9.5 to 1
Carburettor .... 2 Weber 40 DCOE
Fuel pump .... mechanical
Fuel tank .... 9 gallons
Fuel recommended .... super
Valve gear .... dohc
Max. power (gross) .. 115 bhp at 6000 rpm
Max. torque .... 106lb.ft. at 4500 rpm
Specific power output ......73.8 bhp/litre
Electrical system .. 12v, 38 amp hr battery, 264 watt generator.

TRANSMISSION
Four speed manual all synchro gearbox. Single dry plate clutch.

Gear	Ratio	Max/1000 Rpm	Max. mph
Rev	3.324	—	—
1st	.2972	—	38
2nd	2.210	—	58
3rd	1.397	—	84
4th	1.000	17.8	114
Final drive ratio	3.777 to 1		

CHASSIS
Wheelbase ....7ft. 10½in.
Track front .... 4ft. 1in.
Track rear .... 4ft. 2in.
Length ....13ft.
Width .... 5ft. 1¾in.
Height .... 4ft. 5in.
Clearance .... 5¾in.
Kerb weight ....16 cwt. 40lbs.
Weight distribution front/rear51.6/48.4 perce
1b/bhp ....15lb.

SUSPENSION
Front: MacPherson strut independent, telescopic shock absorbers.
Rear: Rigid axle, semi-elliptic leaf spring.
Brakes: Disc/drum servo-assisted; 286 sq. in. of swept area.
Steering .... Rack and pinion.
Turns lock to lock 3.5
Turning circle ....30ft.
Wheels: Steel disc with 165 by 13 tubeless radial ply tyres.

PERFORMANCE
Top speed ....114.1 mph
Average (both ways) ....112.8 mph
Standing quarter mile ....16.8 sec.

Acceleration Zero to	seconds
30 mph	3.6
40 mph	5.2
50 mph	6.7
60 mph	8.6
70 mph	11.4
80 mph	14.7
90 mph	20.7

	3rd	top
20-40 mph	—	—
30-50	4.7	7.8
40-60	4.7	7.0
50-70	5.0	7.8
60-80	5.8	9.2

BRAKING: Five crash stops from 60 mph

Stop	Percent G	Pedal pressure
1	.81	49 lb
2	.80	50
3	.82	51
4	.76	54
5	.75	55

Consumption: 25.4 mph over 418 miles including all tests; 26 mpg in normal country and suburban use.

Speedo error
Indicated mph   30 40 50 60 70 80
Actual mph   29 39 49 59 68 78

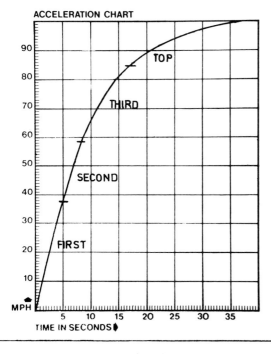

ACCELERATION CHART

TOP
THIRD
SECOND
FIRST

MPH / TIME IN SECONDS ▸

HOW FORD ESCORT T/C COMPARES

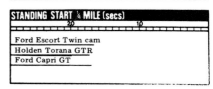

MAXIMUM SPEED (mean) M.P.H.
70 80 90 100 110 120 130
Ford Escort Twin cam ($3,000)
Holden Torana GTR ($2,834)
Ford Capri GT ($3,230)

0-60 M.P.H. SECONDS
25 20 15 10 5
Ford Escort Twin cam
Holden Torana GTR
Ford Capri GT

M.P.G. Overall
10 20 30 40
Ford Escort Twin cam
Holden Torana GTR
Ford Capri GT

STANDING START ¼ MILE (secs)
20 10
Ford Escort Twin cam
Holden Torana GTR
Ford Capri GT

TWO ESCORTS with a lot in common — both are privately owned, prepared and run, both are absolutely immaculate and both are top runners in their field, outperforming comparable works or semi-works cars. And both owners were prepared to put their reputations on the line when they handed over their cars to Rob Luck for a no-limits, no-holds-barred test. This is how he found them . . . .

SLIGHTLY sideways — a rare pose for the Fanning Escort which is normally driven very fast, but very straight by super-cool Bill Fanning. As a complete privateer, Fanning has humbled the mighty works and semi-works Escorts with his professional approach.

ESCORTS

GIANT TWIN
ROAD & RACE TEST

SELDOM straight — and that's normal Escort rally progress. The immaculate Bob Inglis car is set-up for pretty neutral steering with the pleasant option of oversteer for fast trailing-throttle entry, or full-bore power exit.

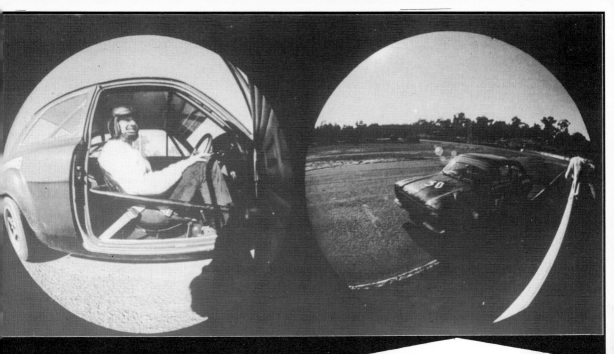

FOR RACE & RALLY

FANNING's action machine — the immaculate dark blue Escort has become a baby legend in Improved Production racing.

INGLIS Escort — flexible rally machine that recently made an easy switch to Rallycross for a series of wins at Catalina Park's new circuit.

FANNING cool — and how it hots up any good Improved Production race. Despite a completely private effort, Fanning has embarrassed the Big Boys with his rapid machine and forceful driving. Here he finds the inside running on Brian Foley's Alfa and Jim McKeown's Porsche at recent Farm meet.

YOU might call Bill Fanning the "Easy Rider" of motor racing. The only major differences between Peter Fonda, and the quietly-spoken demon of Improved Production racing, is that Fanning is more professional, more dedicated, and more successful. His fan club may also be slightly smaller.

But the basic approach has been the same. Enter a field run almost solely on big money, well-established principles and techniques and puffed-up with "experts" and ballyhoo and quietly and simply go about demolishing every known principle (except professionalism). Then beat every last one of them at their own game.

At the end, the aim is the same — to be a box office success. Relatively, Fanning has probably done better than Fonda and Hopper — he started with less and won more, and he's stayed at the top. It's been no easy ride — because doing anything properly never is, but in motor racing, Fanning at least appears to be the ultimate Easy Rider with his super-cool approach.

The measure of most men's success is in results, but for Fanning there's been an extra yardstick — the deepening red glow on the faces of his works and semi-works opposition.

For almost 12 months he has quietly punted his dark blue baby charger round Australian circuits, and disgraced the best efforts of his Escort opposition.

The record alone is enough. Around 15 starts for seven outright wins in Improved Production ... same lap time as Pete Geoghegan's Falcon at Warwick Farm ... consistently 3-4 seconds faster than the semi-works Escorts almost everywhere — (but particularly at the Farm) — and remember that includes FVAs and BDAs ... and even faster than Alan Moffat's full Ford works Sports Shut FVA Escort at Lakeside — 61.1 secs against 62.8.

Now weigh-in a few other factors — money, support, experience.

The Fanning Escort took less than three months to build. The work was done solely by Fanning and the well-respected race-preparation expert, Ian Hindmarsh.

On the track, ready to race, with spare rubber on the trailer its all-up cost was a mere $8300. It's doubtful if the Ford works, Stillwell and Fahey

cars could be costed out at much less than $25,000 — just going on the equipment alone.

Fanning and Hindmarsh started cold with the Escort — no support from anyone, no help, no advice, no free bits, no cheques. And no Escort experience.

Fanning previously raced a Lotus Cortina he prepared largely himself. Hindmarsh's ability is unquestioned — but his knowledge of race Escorts was almost zero at the start.

They attacked the job with a single-minded purpose — to build an out-and-out open-wheeler racing car, then attach an Escort body to it.

And it is that approach which has put them way ahead of every works and semi-works Escort in Australasia — although they're way down on power, financial backing, and even experience.

Hindmarsh and Fanning have total faith in their product — and for good

ESCORTS FOR RACE & RALLY

I REMEMBER noticing the sky was very blue as I hit the jump-up sideways. Then the whole thing got airborne, flying at a crazy angle and finally crunching down on the other side near the dirt verge on two wheels. But the big fat Uniroyals bit hard and with full throttle the car was straightening up before the other side even landed. Then suddenly we were on top of a tight right-hander over a wooden bridge going much too fast and at least two gears too high up.

Off the throttle, very firm and hard once on the picks carefully matching downshifts to the tacho despite being very, very busy. The car was completely sideways now, and the wheel wound round till it seemed there couldn't be any lock left. I finished the slide in the loose gravel on the exit with trailing throttle then flicked over the little wheel and laid into the go-pedal for a full-bore sideslip charge on the opening left-hander on the other side. Rev-and-shift, rev-and-shift up the box and the little beast was already back on the ton and gobbling up the open country ... looking hungrily for some more scary, twisty bits ....

I picked the Bob Inglis car to test for some very good reasons. It's not the only well-prepared Escort running in rallies, and it's not even the most

successful, but it is definitely the best privately built car and it is most consistent. Also its owner was keen to establish whether an impartial driver would find it equally appealing.

I have driven a few rally cars — and among them some of the top cars in the country. The Inglis car is not even nearly the fastest car in rallying, nor does it feel it, but it is probably one of the safest, best balanced and comfortable cars to drive. It is completely predictable, acutely sensitive, and totally progressive in every facet of performance.

It has no vile traits, it seems completely indestructible in the body and quite unburstable in the engine compartment. It can be driven past the limits and brought back again with a cool head behind the wheel, and it would be impossible to attribute any misadventure to anything but driver error.

INGLIS hot seat — the luxury works rally bucket from which Bob Inglis controls one of the most rapid Escort rally machines in Australia.

Its cornering style — the most important aspect of any rally car — can be simply evaluated. Approach the corner if possible too fast, give one hard push on the non-power assisted stoppers. When the outside of the corner starts to look as though it's about to rush up and smack you in the face, get off the brakes very quickly and get it sideways. If the corner approach angle doesn't let it go sideways naturally (rare), handbrake it, or even throttle-oversteer it (very game). Almost as soon as you've wrapped on lock — hit it with full throttle and gun it till you hit the next bend.

There are only three speeds for the Escort anywhere — full throttle, sideways and stopped-in-control. The car is so completely rigid it can be slammed full bore over the toughest country you'll find, and the suspension is so good you don't have

THE EDITOR *squeezes through the tangle of roll cage bars and in behind the tiny SAAS wheel for a snug driving position. He reported magnificent neutral handling and turned in competitive lap times to prove it.*

reason. It is no simple task to take on $60,000 Porsches and Alfas with an $8300 private effort, equal their lap times and constantly nudge, push and embarrass them all round Australian circuits.

It was this faith that led them to hand over the car to me at Sydney's Amaroo Park circuit and instruct me to go as quick as I liked. Said Bill Fanning "Do what you like, see how it'll go. It's OK to push it." And Ian Hindmarsh: "Bill uses 7800 maximum — that should be enough for you".

I fixed-on the Bell Star, bolted into the racing harness and found I fitted much like Wild Willie.

Wheel and pedal reach was just right, and though Bill thought the wide plate on the throttle pedal wouldn't suit my heel-toeing it was perfect. I fired it up, rumbled out of the pits at 3000 without riding the clutch, and settled

into the business of feeding the beast 7800 at every possible opportunity and stopping and turning it just right when corners popped up.

On my second lap, I dropped an easy 59.4 and felt I wouldn't go any faster without getting just a little bit keen in a car that wasn't mine. I did another four laps between 59.4 and 59.7 and called in. The tell-tale was still on 7800.

Bill went out, and did a 58.9 on his third lap and followed it with five more between that and 59.2, and pulled in. Ian Hindmarsh put it on the trailer.

The most remarkable thing about the Fanning Escort is how easy it is to drive. I do not run many track tests, and it was many months previously that I had been on the track.

Yet I was able to step into a car I had never seen before and lap within half a

second of its owner — at a pace comparable with the fastest Improved Production tourer operating in this country.

It really proves how good the car is — because I didn't have to work hard to get the time. It feels exactly and precisely like a racing car in every aspect of driving. It performs best when driven completely smoothly and it will put down record times without ever getting out of a neutral handling state.

It steers and stops just like an open wheeler — progressively and accurately, and it is completely vice-free.

At Amaroo — a dicey circuit for track testing because there's no escape route except dirt bank "launching ramps" — I couldn't have been happier. Even topping Skyline flat and plucking brakes and gears while still cocked over, then slamming down into the tight right-hander of the "bobsled run" it was a simple, effortless affair.

Heading hard into a corner, the little beast needed one hard brake application, matched with downshifts where necessary. The correct line produced gentle understeer if late-braking was applied, but at the apex the car was neutrally on line and power at the right spot produced gentle roll-oversteer that was always completely progressive.

This is because the suspension is set-up with firm front end and soft tail

ESCORTS FOR RACE & RALLY

to feather the throttle — it simply doesn't tramp or dance or hop off line.

The brakes are brilliant — removing the power booster gives firm, progressive stoppers and I've never driven a car that cried out so loud when it wanted you to get off the picks and back on the throttle.

And the engine is completely responsive — no flat spots and no nasty hesitations. It swings that tacho needle right to 6500-7000 and you can match shifts up or down the box against the needle with good accuracy — allowing for needle whiplash.

Like any car in any driving situation, you'll get the best of it by driving completely smoothly all the time. It seems strange to talk of opposite lock and smoothness in the same context, but there's something almost rhythmical about hurling a car around

completely flat out — if you're doing it properly. Brake applications, wheel movements and throttle pressures can all be applied smoothly, keeping the car always in balance and never introducing jerky movements of body, transmission or steering.

But opposed to this smoothness, is the complete brutality you can apply to the Inglis car in tackling tough terrain. While you're wrapped-up in a cockpit, making your smooth driving manoeuvres you can be pounding the car over boulders, potholes, jumps and grids so hard your teeth jar. The car never protests. And, almost unbelievably, it never rattles. Never rattles!

You don't believe me? During a tough and extensive 200 mile workout on some of the nastiest dirt stretches I could find in the short time available,

the only loose noise I heard was the occasional clunk of my camera case in the boot, or the suspension reaching the end of its travel.

Bob Inglis built it that way — and it has stayed that way despite 15,000 miles of gruelling rally, including the Southern Cross and the Dulux. His theory is quite simple — if there are no noises, you can hear a new one as soon as it starts.

Bob Inglis is something of a perfectionist. Nearly 30, and Manager of a Sydney company fabricating sheet plastic, he bought the Escort — the ex-Bill Orr imported racing Twin Cam — from the Alto Ford lot at Gordon. His chief reasons for buying this car when he knew it had already been rolled, were that it was equipped with good seats, 6 in. Minilites, a diff, and a good engine and some other gear that he'd otherwise have paid a whole bag extra for — and at stock Twin Cam list price inclusive the price seemed good.

The car was driven straight to his Lindfield home and into the garage where special stands he had built were bolted-on after the car had been completely stripped. The stands held the car clear of the ground and allowed the entire body to be rotated through 360 degrees. This was essential for him to complete the next stage of preparation — a monumental 80-hour task of welding every seam on the car.

Then followed extensive re-inforcing — plates along the rails running up the

NAVIGATOR's view: *Halda Twinmaster, clock, and battery of switches to control all operations himself. Plastic pipe normally runs to big water reservoir for high-output electric pump.*

with only one degree of camber change throughout the front-end movement.

I tried for full-bore oversteer exits a couple of laps in the Cutting and on the Hairpin. The car was delightfully controllable with steering and throttle and any suggestion of accidental over-correction seemed impossible.

After my six laps on the limit, I felt ready for another hundred — the car was so comfortable and relaxing to drive. This is typical of the Fanning/Hindmarsh attitude to construction and preparation — they both believe complete driver comfort is essential.

The buckets are ex-Works Lotus Cortina with matched-up full aircraft-style harness — and the ever-present protection of the massive looming rollcage all around (it was built by Colin Bond).

The legs can stretch out virtually straight to the pedals with good thigh support and just at wrist-reach is the fat little thick-grip SAAS wheel which I passed onto Fanning after he spotted it in my own private Escort.

Instrumentation in the Twin Cam's binnacle now comprises a mechanical tachometer for absolute accuracy, an unconnected electrical tacho in the opposite spot ("just to fill the hole") fuel pressure gauge on top and combined oil pressure and water temperature gauge below.

A small steel projection over on the dash contains master switch for the ignition/fuel supply, warning light and amp meter. There's a fire extinguisher under your legs and apart from that, the cockpit looks quite standard.

And that's in definite contrast to what goes on *underneath* the body.

The car started life as a bare body shell from Alto Ford at Gordon. It was shipped to Hindmarsh's Artarmon workshop and the body completely sand-blasted, and strengthened in potential trouble spots. Every seam was welded.

Then all the guards were cut-off, and brand new English Ford competition "flares" fitted. This was a major operation because it requires reconstruction of the inner guards which don't match the new ones, and the "flares" themselves have to be shaped to wheel clearance requirements, etc. — they come as complete "blanks" for individual owners to hand-tailor.

Fibreglass boot and bonnet lids were fabricated and perspex windows installed in all apertures except the windscreen, where laminate was fitted.

Then the real work began underneath. The rear suspension was completely redesigned on open-wheeler principles. Hindmarsh and Fanning knew the English Broadspeed Escorts with their Watts linkage/four-radius rod system were the best but they had no guide-lines.

They had to experiment, and they

VEGANTUNE/LUCAS injection gear on top of BRM head for a healthy 140-plus bhp, and some special Hindmarsh/Fanning tweaks. Now the car is scheduled to get 1850cc Waggott FVA for sports closed.

built special mounting brackets on axle housing and body to take fully-adjustable rose-jointed radius rods and linkages.

The lateral Watts linkage is located on the diff housing, and to avoid a massive and heavy structure they gave positive lightweight location by bracing the diff and mounting against the hubs. The diff casing itself was hardened.

(Continued on page

firewalls, and in every other stress point that would need extra strength to stop bending when bottoming or landing from punishing jumps.

Then came the big injection — 20 lbs of high density 2lb mix foam forced into the box-frame chassis rails, door sills and other pockets, for added strength and rigidity.

Then slowly and carefully the bits were dropped back in. The engine was completely stripped, found to be in excellent condition and carefully rebuilt in its near-standard form. A big stay was fixed across the tops of the inner front guards to stop them bowing in.

Underneath, the McPherson struts were bolted home, after welding-on close-fit steel tube on the base of the mounts and filling them with Koni adjustable shockers. The tops of the strut mounts were also extensively re-inforced. English competition rally coils were used, and the front stabiliser bar was double-mounted at every point, and the locating rubbers trimmed for better fit to reduce movement.

Down at the rear end, four-leaf standard Escort springs replaced the three-leaf Twin Cams and they were bolted up to the Salisbury diff with spring hanger plates re-inforced by ¾ in. x ½ in. bar — to stop bending which loosens the U-bolts.

The location of the rear shockers wasn't moved — some drivers relocate them upright — but they were replaced with Konis. Also, the subframe that locates the shockers to the body was strengthened and the rubber noise-isolation rubbers sandwiched between mounts and body were removed for a solid fit.

Bob Inglis also removed the small locating stays on the diff and threw them away. Rally experience has proved they do not provide additional location under tough conditions and they tend to break. However a K-Mac stabiliser bar was fitted for additional rear-end location. The entire suspension was jacked up — the rear sitting higher than the front to provide roll oversteer handling.

The differential itself was carefully rebuilt. Rally practice has proved that more backlash is necessary for gruelling rally work than normal road use, and this was built-in to the differential to stop it chewing itself out. It produces a definite whine at some speeds — but this is no concern in a rally machine.

Further forward in the transmission line, the gearbox was also completely rebuilt with a few of Bob's own personal "tweaks" to ensure long life and minimise failures.

Next job was a complete roll cage — which Col Bond and George Shepheard built into the cockpit — eventually extending the rails into the boot when it was found the tail started to "drop" after some hard rally use. Local rally rules prevent the roll bar

running outside the body like the English Escorts, but Inglis found the overall design worked well.

Wiring was a major project. The entire car was re-wired by Inglis to his own specifications — and every item has its own fuse. This even includes separate headlight fuses — this prevents complete shorting of the light system if, say, the left side of the car biffs a tree or bank and knocks out one light.

The car is also equipped with a battery master switch on the rear floor

(Continued on page

MASSIVE light pack, fat Minilites and tyres and purposeful paintjob show off the Escort's style in sideways action on tight dirt hairpin.

FRESH NEW STYLING, RIDE REFINEMENTS AND MOST IMPORTANT OF ALL — MORE MPG !

FORD'S Escort re-hash will have serious ramifications in the Australian small car market. In the battle against Japanese imports the new small Ford must have the goods. London Editor 'Dev' Dvoretsky previews the new range and says the '75 Escort is quieter, more comfortable and more economical to run.

FORD'S NEW Escort package we scoop-previewed in the February issue comes in three basic shapes, four basic engines, nine basic trims and nineteen different models. It is slightly shorter, slightly wider, slightly higher and weighs more than the previous model.

It has much more soundproofing so is quieter, it has a bigger boot, twenty-three percent more glass area and is slightly slower — but it does more precious kilometres to the litre of higher priced 97 octane.

It is better finished than its predecessor, handles better, is more comfortable and with services only every 10,000 kilometres should be extremely cheap to maintain (either at your garage or by your own handywork!)

Although as I write I don't know the exact price, I do know it's going to be dearer to buy in the first place. All in all it's not a bad package, more sophisticated than the previous model in some respects — simpler in others. Like the Capri Two launched just a year ago it reflects Ford's sensitivity to the market trend for more "complete" cars even at the smaller end of the scale.

The detail to soundproofing and

THE NEW Escort lineup will consist of two-door and four-door sedans plus a three-door station wagon. The new range is on-sale in the UK and will probably come to Australia in July/August this year. Mechanicals are identical to the current model, but body styling and trim is all-new.

seating comfort show Ford's consciousness that in the tougher times ahead some motorists will probably be going just down-market to what they were driving before, yet still wanting the quietness and comfort of the car they've just left.

All three bodies — two and four-door and three-door wagons — progress the seventies line with slightly dipped flat shelf bonnets, slab sides and semi fastback rears. Ford says it's an international design — another of the "world" cars this magazine mooted some years back (the first anywhere to do so).

Basically the design is much the same as those from Fiat, GM, Chrysler et-al, yet all have their distinctive differences so that the more observant can single them out in the crowd. The four basic engines are the now familiar Ford 'Kent' series (including for the first time two models powered by the 1598,, version used in the Ford Mexico). The engines all share the same 80.98mm bores but have different strokes. They use a five bearing crank, cast iron block with cast iron cylinder head, in-line vertical valves operated by pushrods and rockers, with a camshaft is chain driven at the side.

The 1097cc 1100 HC/basic unit has a 53.29mm stroke, an uprated from 8:1 to 9:1 compression ratio, and now delivers 35.3kW at 5500rpm instead of the previous 34.5kW at 6000rpm.

ALTHOUGH all styling was carried out in the German studios the up-market versions carry a Ghia badge on the tail to give the Escort more continental appeal. The most significant factor about the new body is the vastly increased glass area.

FORD'S FIGHTING CHANCE

COCKPIT styling is very basic (this is the Sport version), but seats and trim differ widely. Luxury models will get cloth trim on the seats, carpets and additional soundproofing. Dash function controls are all in the same place as before, but there is slightly more room in the front compartment.

Torque is the same at 73.5kW at 3000rpm. The 1300 HC unit (1297cc) has a stroke of 62.99mm, an uprated to 9.2:1 compression ratio, but delivers the same power 42kW at 5500rpm and 91.6Nm at 3000rpm.

The GT version of the same engine, with a twin choke Weber (a single choke Ford carb is used on the 1100 HC and 1300 HC) delivers 51.5kW at 5500rpm (down from 53.7kW at 6000rpm) and 92.2Nm at 4000rpm. Top-of-the-range 1600GT (1598cc) has a stroke of 77.62mm, a compression ratio of 9:1 and with the smaller twin choke Weber delivers 61.8kW at 5500rpm — again down on the previous version which gave 64kW at 6000 rpm. Torque is 124.5Nm at 3500rpm.

All the engines are rated to the strict and carefully controlled German DIN standard and meet the current European emission requirements.

That excellent all-synchro four-speed manual box with it's light change has been further improved with the fitting of a 19.05cm diameter clutch on all models. The GT versions of the 1300 and 1600 units fitted to the Sport and Ghia 'luxury' models use a special set of close ratios with higher first and second gears. For this more rigorous application, the unit is uprated by shot-peening of the gear set and the use of high capacity ball bearings and modified needle bearings for the gear cluster.

For the first time Ford offers a special version of the C3 automatic transmission. This new version of the C3 has been specially engineered for the range to cut down transmission losses (consumption figures for the auto seem to bear this out). A special heat exchanger built into the bottom of the engine radiator allows the transmission oil to warm up quicker and therefore a smaller torque converter housing is needed, with much reduced oil capacity — and the lubricant never needs changing!

Ford have done almost five million kilometres of testing, · including 750,000km on their Belgium test track with the new transmission. Tests included a de-bogging cycle in mud where the car rocked back and forth between drive and reverse 300 times. A bump test with the transmission in park utilised a three ton truck running away on a one in five gradient and bumping into the Escort!

The transmission is ultra smooth and features "zero-throttle braking" whereby intermediate and low are selected in turn on the over-run below 32km/h to give better control at low speed without having to use the manual over-ride.

Low can be engaged manually for emergency braking below 64km/h.

Ford has decided to go over entirely to steel-braced radial ply tyres. The suspension — still MacPherson at the front with a live axle and leaf springs at the rear — has been refined to cope with the extra harshness and bump-thump of the radials.

The MacPherson Struts now have an increased diameter stabilizer bar and more progressive bump rubbers. Rear axle location is aided by a short anti-roll bar and vertical telescopic dampers (similar to those introduced in the 1973 Capri). Rear leaf springs are wider (5.8cm instead of 5cm) enabling a cut from four leaves to three. On the Sport version rates are stiffer, the ride height is an average of .8cm lower and low profile and wider, 175/70 tyres on 5J rims are standard. Station wagon versions use the old rear suspension to allow for greater tray width.

Sport Escorts have front discs as standard and these are 2.5cm larger in diameter and use pads 30percent larger in area and 50percent larger in volume to extend service life. On Sport and Ghia models a vacuum servo is standard and, like the discs, are available as an option on all models. Cars with drum brakes get 12in wheels with radials on 4.5C rims. Disc-braked cars get 13in wheels with 155 section radials on 4.5C rims, except for the Sport and Ghia which have the sports-styled 5Js.

Internally the new Escorts range from basic to luxury — the top-of-the-range Ghia is big car comfort in a small car package which Ford reckons European (and world) buyers will now be crying out for.

Seats of the upline versions — there are nine different trims from the basic to the Ghia — are even better than before with adjustable squabs and cloth coverings available as options.

MODERN MOTOR — MARCH 1975

THIS SCHEMATIC exposes all, but the main changes in running gear revolve around subtle suspension differences and better isolation from road shock.

All versions now have carpet on the floor — yes, even the basic model, which until now has been offered with rubber.

All versions have a completely new fascia — simple yet really efficient. The instrument cluster is right in front of the driver and contains a good large speedo with easy-to-read figures with (on the Sport and Ghia models) a similar-sized dial on the left for the tacho. The whole cluster is sealed with an angled lens to minimize reflections (the Sport and Ghia have a trip recorder).

Ford's very good aeroflow ventilation system now has its rear outlet in the rear quarter pillars (instead of at the base of the rear window).

Boot area is up ten percent to 292 litres and the extra glass area makes up 25kg of the cars' added overall weight. Two-speed wipers are used throughout the range and seat frames on all cars are now mounted on sliding runners. Redesign of the rear seats increases leg room by a handy five centimetres.

To eliminate drive-line induced harshness or boom from the longer-stroke 1600 engine versions Ford have fitted a two-piece prop shaft with a constant velocity centre joint with bonded support bearing. The 1600 engine is not available in the station wagon variant.

Other refinements include the insulation of the clutch release fulcrum pin to prevent rattle during idling in neutral.

A small 'bib' spoiler is incorporated in the front apron to make for better stabilisation in cross winds. Rear brakes are now self-adjusting and all versions, with the exception of the base models, come equipped with a heated rear screen as standard.

While overall top speeds are slightly down they're still way above the legal limit everywhere except for Germany! The basic 1100 can top 134km/h, get to 100km/h in 25.7 seconds. Do 50-100km/h in 29.7sec in top gear and return a healthy 8.37litres/100km consumption. The top-of-the-range 1600 Ghia and 1600 Sports have top speeds of 162km/h, get to 100km/h in 13 secs, and take only 18 secs for the 50-100km/h time while returning 9.6litres/100km.

Even the automatic versions don't do badly. The 1300 auto does 135km/h top speed and takes 24.9 secs to reach 100km/h. Touring consumption is 9.4litres/100km. The 1600 Sport and Ghia automatic versions have a top speed of 159km/h, get to 100km/h in around 15.4 sec. and return 9.6litres/100km.

There'll be an RS1800 version of the new Escort with the bored 1840 BDA alloy rally engine, giving 93kW (DIN) at 6500rpm, 193km/h top speed and a 0-100km time of eight seconds. The two-litre works version of this engine produces 171kW at 8200rpm for rallying, or 205kW at 8200rpm for circuit use. Ford will later introduce an RS2000 version with OHC Cortina power-plant under the bonnet. 🅗

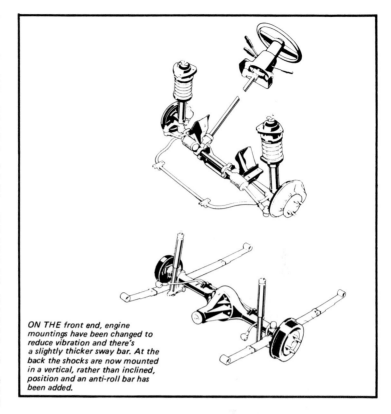

ON THE front end, engine mountings have been changed to reduce vibration and there's a slightly thicker sway bar. At the back the shocks are now mounted in a vertical, rather than inclined, position and an anti-roll bar has been added.

THE NEW body has allowed a little more luggage space in the boot. Fuel tank intrudes on the right and the spare rides upright on the left.

PERFORMANCE

	Top speed km/h	0-100km/h secs	50-100km/h secs (top gear)	Fuel consumption l/100km (cruising)
1100	133	25.7	29.7	8.3 (34mpg)
1300	140	22.9	22.9	9.4 (30mpg)
1300 auto	135	24.9	NA	10.1 (28mpg)
1300 Sport	151	16.3	20	9.5 (30mpg)
1600 Sport	162	13	17	8.7 (32mpg)
1600 Sport auto	159	15.4	NA	9.6 (29mpg)

DIMENSIONS

Overall length:	405.8cm
width:	159.6cm
height:	138.4cm
Wheelbase:	240.7cm
Track — front:	125.8cm
rear:	128.4cm
Weights: 1100 — 839kg, 1300 — 860kg, 1600 Sport — 892kg, 1600 GHIA — 906kg (916 with auto).	
Fuel Tank Capacity:	41 litres

Testing the ESCORT II/RS1800...

RS-REFINED

ABOVE: The RS1800 comes as a two-door, with luxury trim which includes special wheels and rear spoiler. LEFT: The dash layout is identical to the base-line cars, except for tacho and some additional gauges. Plus there's a sporty steering wheel, special seats and centre console. FAR RIGHT: RS1600 — this is the car the RS1800 replaces. The 1600 and a number of other special models carried off a great many victories for FordSport teams around the world. Correspondent Andrews says the RS1800 is a 'boulevarde special' compared to the old 1600.

RIGHT: This is a specially tricked-up version to show what the car looks like in rally trim. After early successes in British rallies Ford expects big things of the RS1800 in competition.

THE ASSIGNMENT seemed straight-forward enough — just drive and compare the recently released Escort RS 1800 to the RS 1600, its predecessor. But actually it became more — it became a report on a breed of car that is soon to vanish due to legislation and assorted ecological problems. The report had to be relative in terms of today's thinking, and with this in mind I felt need to be more critical of the new car than perhaps I would have been a year ago.

When the RS 1600 was released over five years ago it was a real fireball rock-it-to-me mini road burner. Today with new values (and price structures), its lack of refinement couldn't really be justified because new cars are being released that have that blistering performance with acceptable road manners. "Horror!'', cry the enthusiasts bemoaning the gradual disappearance of real drivers' cars. But we have to be realists — the writing *is* on the wall. Ford has even finally realised this and decided to update its high performing bombshell. In fact one gathers that the only reason Ford still makes the RS model is so it can

homologate its tweaked (up to 220 BHP) versions for people like Dave Brodie (now into Capris) and Roger Clark — who is already successfully campaigning his BDA.

Well the new car is quite frankly a disappointment — this new kid on the block is actually the same old recipe dressed-up in a new wrapper. It's the direct development of the BDA 1600 MK II (with the alloy block and head) which was the road-going version of the Cosworth FVA F2 engine. Why disappointing? Well, to answer this best, refer to the chart overleaf. In a straight comparison with other competitive models the RS 1800 doesn't fare well at all. Where once there was no direct equivalent now there are too many — and the old recipe just doesn't cut the mustard any more! By end of 1971 the RS 1600 cost £stg1517 — less than four years later it nearly doubles its price to £stg2900.

Some things have changed noticeably in that time. Where as once you had to be a really avid sports car driver to enjoy the RS 1600, today its revitalised brother is more civilised — but not much! The old model was

probably the most uncompromising product ever to be publicly offered by a major manufacturer. Yet for all its rip-snorting hypertension and temperament the car was still a good basic platform for serious racers to work on. It was too tame to race off the showroom floor yet not really suitable for modern traffic conditions.

Today the RS 1800 is even harder to justify when it isn't even the quickest in its class! In fact unless it's bought to build into your special-stage rally supercar (which it does become) it becomes superfluous even in Ford's own lineup as the newly released Capri 'S' 3000 GT out-performs it for more than £stg400 less money — and the Escort still hasn't the looks or tne pose value of the all-black hatch-back V6.

So where does it leave the RS 1800? More sophisticated cars like the Lancia Beta Coupe, Alfetta 180C, Fiat 124, R17 Gordini and Scirocco either outperform it or underprice it — or both! And dig the Celica GT price tag in UK. Twin cams, 5-speed box et al, need I go on . . . In face even though the Citroen CX2000 is in a different category I could not resist the price

SPEEDSTER, OR RALLY SPECIAL?

HOT BEHIND the release of the 'cooking' Escort II comes the sporty RS1800 version, and Ford have delivered it into a highly competitive market area up against cars like the Scirocco, Alfasud Ti and Lancia Beta. How does it shape up? Our roving European correspondent Paul Andrews says only just . . .

ESCORT II/RS1800

comparison by listing it — a mere £stg205 more.

But enough diversions, most people buy the RS 1800 for its performance so let's investigate the powerplant and how it motivates. It has an alloy block and head whereas the original RS 1600 had an iron block. The old bore and stroke was 80.98 x 77.62 now it's 86.75 x 77.62 mm for 1840cc. The dual 40 DCOEs have been replaced by one dual choke (progressive) 32/36 DCAV Weber which accounts for 86kW at 6500, down 3.7kW on the old car. Torque is up though with 163Nm at 4000rpm — the RS 1600 and 150Nm at 4500. All this has made the engine more civilised but taken away the old car's punch, as the 1800 suffocates at 6000 rpm sounding very asthmatic and coarse. Down low it shines, yet neither car is still happy in top gear at less than 50-60km/h.

The old car was meant to be blasted around, in high revs and on the cam.

The new car with the changes, plus 30km/h per 1000rpm top gearing (old car was 27.5) and extra weight has lost its sparkle. The 1800 also has a lower compression — down to 9:1, which actually helps cold weather starts and staying in tune. One thing is for sure though, and that is you can pick the heritage of the reskinned car. All one has to do is open the bonnet to see the same old inner panels — and it still is not self-suporting on a £stg3000 car!

Engine access to the ancillaries is worse than before even though the dual Weber manifold is gone — because the car now has a big air cleaner (and silencer) complete with temperature controlled intake that limits work space.

The handling has had a little attention, but its not really 1975 stuff. The suspension is specially stiffened with Armstrong competition struts at front and Girling gas-filled dampers and radius arms at back. This is the basic difference between your new RS 1800 and 1600 sport models. Now with the South Ockendon operation (AVO) closed the RS model goes into mainstream production at Halewood. The rack and pinion steering has always been good and accurate — though it now hasn't the old kickback problem. Handling is fairly precise and predictable but it didn't appeal to me, having been spoilt on cars like the Alfasud Ti — a car that has phenomenal roadholding but not at the expense of its ride characteristics. The old RS1600 was a "jaw-breaker", and the new car isn't a great deal better!

The Pirelli CN36 175/70 x 13 on wide rims obviously have something to do with its attitudes for they are particularly adhesive and at slow speeds hide the understeer. Only once near the limits can you tell because you are working! The nose runs wide and will break away first, back off and you're in business again but watch the wet roads and roundabouts. Whereas the old car virtually enticed you to rush around "hanging the tail out", displaying ragged-edge antics for cornering thrills, the RS 1800 is not as quick but does its job with less fuss until you reach its limits.

Then it goes messy and you have to act seriously or it can become quite unenjoyable, particularly if, as in Australia, owners basically are used to cars that require opposite lock. The stability on the open road is much better than the RS 1600 as it's not

affected by crosswinds or surface irregularities — possibly an aerodynamic factor as one car is very rounded, the other rather square and stiff. Ford engineers have made the rear suspension softer and increased the roll stiffness at the front which has resulted in a calculated understeer nearly all the time. The old car went from mild understeer to controlled oversteer; — definitely hairy but most rewarding if that's your bag (as it used to be mine!)

The gearbox is the German-built single-rail shift with shot-peened internals (this box, minus the 'nicer' ratios is used on the Mustang II and Pinto). The RS 1800 through the gears gets 58-106-153--182km/h — not as close as the older version, which peaked second at 93km/h and third around 145km/h for a smoother, more correct flow pattern. Both boxes, nevertheless, are fun to use with positive action, although the old one was a little smoother and the syncros unbeatable.

The brakes still have the same surface area but they work much better (or seem to) and the pressure is definitely less. The Pirellis have a lot to do with the braking capacity, which uplifts the Escort to an excellent rating. Other tests at MIRA have shown 1g deceleration readings with no fade after up to 20 stops from speed with less than five percent pressure increase. That's no comparison for the RS 1600, which needed a heavy, size-thirteen boot. The old car needed the four-wheel-disc kit that was available, or twin boosters.

Once inside the car some features become immediately obvious — the airy feeling with 23percent more glass and a lower beltline and slimmer pillars

Car	Cost	C.C.	kW	G/box	Top speed	0-100 time	400M	mpg	length (cm)	width (cm)	boot (cu.ft.)	Power to weight ratio (kg/kW)
1971 RS 1600	£1517	1601	89.5	4	185	8.45	16.65	26-29	396	152	8.0	10.7
1975 RS 1800	£2990	1840	83.5	4	182	8.7	16.9	26-29	396	154	8.9	11.9
Lancia Beta Coupe	£2697	1756	82.8	5	190	9.0	17.2	25-30	401	166	9.5	12.9
Alfetta	£2970	1779	90.2	5	180	9.5	17.3	24-28	429	163	11.5	13.1
Capri 'S'	£2543	2994	103	4	198	8.4	16.5	20-25	427	169	7.2	12.5
Fiat 124 coupe	£2676	1756	85	5	179	9.2	17.6	26-31	411	167	6.8	13.1
Celica GT/S	£2345	1588	82	5	182	9.3	17.2	26-30	419	163	8.0	12.3
R17 Gordini	£2896	1605	80	5	180	9.8	17.5	27-32	427	163	11.0	14.2
Alfa 2000 GTV	£2999	1962	112	5	185	8.9	16.8	21-27	409	160	6.8	11.1
Dolomite sprint	£2937	1988	95	5	186	8.4	16.7	23-27	413	154	9.4	11.5
Vauxhall Firenza	£3048	2279	98	5	190	8.3	16.5	19-24	427	163	10.5	11.4
BMW 2002	£2999	1990	75	4	175	9.4	17.3	24-27	427	156	7.2	13.4
Datsun 240 K	£2678	2392	97	4	180	9.7	17.3	21-26	442	163	11.0	13.4
VW Scirocco	£2392	1971	64	4	175	9.4	17.5	27-34	389	162	9.0	13.4
Citroen CX 2000	£3195	1998	76	4	180	11.0	18.0	25-31	461	175	12.5	16.6

MODERN MOTOR — NOVEMBER 1975

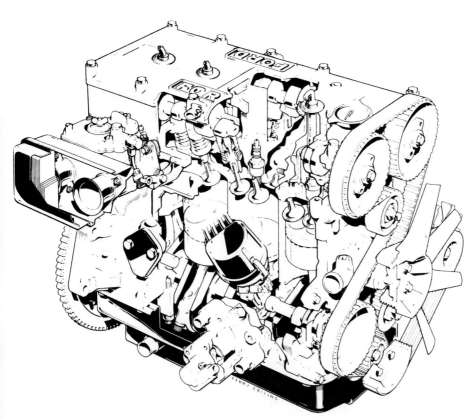

are all good features. The instrument panel is greatly improved but as yet hasn't a totally-integrated look — the ashtray and radio still seem like afterthoughts. The award-winning instrument cluster is fine, not suffering the RS 1600 problem of the steering wheel hiding the secondary instruments — yet the speedo doesn't have km/h readings!

The new interior is better — the RS 1600 was too basic. The buckets of the RS 1800, strangely, aren't as good as the *road* seats on the new 1600 Sport which have been put up for a design award (they deserve it). The RS Escorts always have been 2+2s due to the big rally seats. These recliners just take up too much room, losing the 2in space gain the reworked package (the base cars don't suffer this problem).

There is a lot of space in the cabin, but with cars like the Alfasud around it's not over-generous by comparison. These big front seats, for all their *looks* and size, actually are too low, lack underthigh support for very tall drivers, and the bolsters are too wide for slim drivers.

The RS 1800 now has the Cortina stalks on the column, a big improvement: left for headlight flasher and horn, right has washer/wiper and lights, but they are located too close to each other. Also the fiddly rocker switches of the old car have been re-sorted so that you don't grope in the dark for them!

On the road the new car is less noisy, but it's no LTD. Noise and Vibration Harshness (NVH) has been improved

over the RS 1600, which was like a fire-breathing dragon with a hangover. Wind noise grows at speed, particularly due, I think, to the seals at the top of the doors lifting. At 90mph the exhaust still drones enough so you can't hear the radio. The old car at this stage was like a summit conference at the UN between ermergent nations! The halogen lights are good, yet the car doesn't get the extra lights that are featured on the 1600 sport. The wipers are efficient in the rain, as is the demisting and heating. The heater's booster fan is still too noisy. The fresh air vents now actually do a good job — excellent compared to the old car.

Some random thoughts: finish and fittings of the RS 1800 are better — so they should be for the money and competition it's up against. The doors click shut now and general quality is improving — the quality controllers have a big responsibility. The car doesn't feel like £stg3000 worth — its not obviously luxuriously fitted, rather it's sensible — like a mid-range German car. The striping and spoilers don't really suit the boxy uninspired design that looks (so help me God) like it was styled in Tokyo or Osaka! The car will sell because it offends nobody but there's the easy way out, right? Good for sales, I guess. The bumpers I thought were especially treated chip-resistant epoxy painted, but I've seen Escorts with scratched bumpers already and it reveals chrome-plating underneath!

One sensible improvement is that the

new car only needs one key — not three; door, ignition, boot as before.

In summary, the car probably will sell well because it's a Ford, has a fairly good dealer service backup, parts aren't scarce, you can get a ton of 'trick' bits for it and build up a 200kW road, rally or circuit car and really it still is rapid — it just doesn't have that much breathing space to sit on its laurels! I guess people in UK don't really check around before buying. I was stunned after doing my research into the RS 1800's competitors as to the fantastic selection that's now available for similar money. Now, after this report — the figures in the chart speak for themselves — even though I enjoy blasting down narrow country lanes at sunrise holding good rpm in the gears, I can't honestly say that the Escort would be choice 'numero uno'. Best value would go to the Celica or Datsun. Best performance to the Lancia, Capri or Firenza, most fascinating to the CX 2000. And, one can't overlook the potential of cheaper cars like the Scirocco or Alfa Ti.

So where does this leave the new RS 1800? Only you, Mr Potential Buyer, can really answer this and what you decide will shape future trends. A lot can happen to an 'open' category in four years, Mr Ford, er, Mr Ford . . . I said. What's that? You might drop the RS model and introduce a turbo V6 Capri? Like the Broadspeed? . . . now you're talking. If you can't match the competition on technical sophistication you cover them in tyre smoke! Ⓗ

GOOD GHIA

FORD HAS given itself a whole bunch of headaches with the introduction of the Ghia version of the new Escort. This up-market small car with cloth seats, top-level trim, 1600cc motor, AM/FM radio and vinyl roof was supposed to quietly sit alongside the new XL and L versions and simply 'be available' if a prospective Escort buyer wanted something better than what the company was offering with the base range. That's not entirely true — actually the men at Broadmeadows want to sell as many of whatever they

can get on the dealers' floors and if it's a Ghia Escort at $4420, fine.

So what, you might say. The problem is that the Ghia has rocketed to early success and dealers are way behind in orders. After a few hundred kilometres of L/XL motoring we can understand why buyers want the up-market car. They appreciate the added flexibility and performance which the 1600cc engine gives. It's as simple as that. Our recent survey of Ford dealers (undercover, of course) proves that buyers are driving the cheaper models, then trying the Ghia

and finally *trying* to buy the four-grand special. The dealer then politely tells the customer that he can go on a long waiting list until more stock arrives, or he can have an XL immediately.

When production began the build percentage was 60/40, in favour of the cheaper models. Ford would like it to go 50/50, or even 40/60, but supply of parts, panels and transmissions is the problem. Most, if not all the bits, are sourced out of the British Ford works at Dagenham — and we all know how industrious and hard-working British

HERE'S A new kind of small car. The Escort Ghia is a lightweight package loaded with extra equipment and offers for the first time in Australia all the luxury normally associated with the topline Fairlanes and LTDs. Only poor quality control can destroy this car's excellent chance of success . . . .

MODERN MOTOR — FEBRUARY 1976

car workers are. So here we have a car in a totally unique market slot with buyers panting and straining to spend money and the poor old Ford company has to turn them away — goodness, what'll happen to the profits?

There is no doubt the Ghia is an excellent car. Our only complaints with the base models are the gutless 1300cc engine, inconsistent finish, lack of rear seat legroom and headroom.

The base models will get the 1600cc engine (with single barrel carby) as of next July (in order to comply with ADR 27a on emissions), the finish will improve with time (won't it?) and the back of the front seats (on the L/XL) will be re-shaped to provide more legroom and as a bonus a little more headroom. But the Ghia has everything right now. The seats are superbly comfortable and are finished in a top quality Savannah cloth — how long you can keep it clean remains to be seen. The finish on our test car was so-so. There were runs in the paint, an ill-fitting dashboard, a heater vent which couldn't be closed, ill-fitting boot carpet (more on that later), badly-fitted door trims, loose PK screws in the door frames and an insistent whistle from somewhere underneath.

The equipment level of the Ghia makes it well and truly worth the money — you get the cloth-trimmed seats, AM/FM radio, clock, tacho, vinyl roof, heated rear screen, five inch sports wheels, halogen headlamps, steel-belted radial ply tryes, lockable glove box, day/night rear vision mirror, remote control driver's door mirror, dual horns, laminated windscreen and passenger's door rear-vision mirror. All that for $4420 and you get the big (two-barrel carb)

GHIA has three column-mounted stalks — but they are laid out in reverse positions (flashers left/wipers right) and the third stalk (the headlight control) is badly placed and can be 'knocked-on' by the driver's knee. Dashboard includes a tacho and clock as standard and illuminated heater controls. Pedal placement is okay, but in manual cars the clutch is too close to the centre tunnel and the left foot has to be lifted off the pedal and sits underneath, which is quite awkward. The boot (above right) is roomy and functional — note upright spare placement. The fuel tank is too small for long tours. Seats are very comfortable, but long rearwards travel on the front seats threatens rear seat legroom. Rear seat headroom is not good for super-tall occupants.

ROAD TEST DATA & SPECIFICATIONS

Manufacturer: . . . . .Ford Motor Co. of Australia Broadmeadows
Make/Model: . . . . Escort Ghia
Body type: . . . . .4-door sedan
Test car supplied by: . . . . .Ford Motor Co., Broadmeadows.

ENGINE
Location: . . . . Front
Cylinders: . . . . four-in-line
Bore & Stroke: . . . . .80.98 mm x 77.62 mm
Capacity: . . . . 1598 cc
Compression: . . . . 9.0 to 1
Aspiration: . . . . Single Weber two-barrel carburettor
Fuel pump: . . . . Mechanical
Valve gear: . . . . .OHV
Maximum power: . . . . .131 kW @ 6000 rpm
Maximum torque: . . . . 137 Nm @ 4000 rpm

TRANSMISSION
Type/locations: . . . . Ford C3 three-speed automatic transmission, T-bar shifter
Driving wheels: . . . . Rear

Gear	Gearbox Ratio
1st	2.474
2nd	1.474
3rd	1.00
Final drive:	3.54 to 1

SUSPENSION
Front suspension: . . . . Independent by McPherson strut with anti-roll bar
Rear suspension: . . . . .Live rear axle, semi-elliptic springs with radius arms and anti-roll bar
Shock absorbers: . . . . Direct-acting telescopic
Wheels:13 x 5 styled steel type
Tyres: . . . . YR78S x 13 steel-belt radials

STEERING
Type: . . . . .Rack and pinion
Turns lock to lock: 3.5
Wheel diameter: . . . . 380 mm
Turning circle: . . . . 8.9 m

BRAKES
Front: . . . . Disc — Diameter: 243.8mm
Rear: . . . . Disc — Diameter: 228.6mm
Servo assistance: . . . . Vacuum standard

DIMENSIONS AND WEIGHT
Wheelbase: 2400mm
Overall length: 3978mm
width: 1595mm
height: 1384mm
Track, front: 1257mm
rear: 1283mm
Ground clearance: 125mm
Kerb weight: 950kg

motor which gives the Ghia the necessary punch. On the comfort side there are absolutely excellent door armrests, soft-feel steering wheel, great wads of sound-deadening material, top quality cut-pile carpet, tinted windows, boot light and fully-illuminated heater controls.

The Ghia is well-equipped and very well-priced. The first, most important, most obvious aspect of the new Escort is its incredible quietness and smoothness. The suspension is beautifully damped, there is a complete lack of road noise, engine noise and serious wind noise. The designer, Mr Uwe Bahnsen, stressed the great lengths his engineers went to in order to cut out all unnecessary noise, vibration and harshness. They have totally succeeded.

Ford has been able to inject big car luxury into a light car package and if this is the shape of things to come from Ford then things is lookin' up. If only it can keep up a high quality of finish — its record is not good on that count.

On the finish side we were very

disappointed with several items. The heater control panel looked like it had been fitted by a cross-eyed chimp. It was in no way square in its supposed mounting and you could see light (for the illumination of the controls) shining between the cracks. Also, there was no way of shutting off the air vent. Despite repeated training by Ford PR men in how to close the vent we never succeeded. Eventually we selected the 'Defrost' position and blew uncomfortably cold air up to the screen rather than have it blowing on the occupant's feet.

The boot carpet looked like the guy who fitted it stood back about six feet from the car and threw it into the boot with a carefree over-the-shoulder stroke. The carpeted boot (!) consists of a square of carpet placed neatly (at first) on the floor of the boot — no retaining clips or snaplocks — no nothing. Consequently, after a few kilometres it ends up scrunched-up underneath whatever we're carrying. We got sick of trying to track down the loose PK screws in the driver's door and gave up. First few kilometres in the test car showed up very bad out-of-balance front wheels — these were checked and some adjustment was made but it wasn't really much better. Maybe it was that vicious 'Force Variation' problem which Ford Australia seems destined to contend with into infinity. They've got it on the six-cylinder Cortinas, so I hope it won't be chronic on the Ghias. It could spoil a lovely romance.

On the road we fell in love with the Ghia's touring ability. It's just so beautifully quiet and easy to push along. There is really no effort to putting away long distances in a single bound. It's a refreshing car to drive and the manual Ghia would be a real gem — if we ever see any. Apparently

the manual box which mates to the 1600 2V motor is in shorter supply than Rocking Horses S ... (oops, sorry) and the manual Ghias are delayed in production — a real shame.

We've been talking to the Ford guys about the new Escort for some time and they were all excited about it — but if they were so fired-up about what a great little car it was and how it would sell, then they should have got themselves a little better organised in the supply department. Anyone with half an eye for a sophisticated light car would have seen the Escort (and especially the Ghia) was going to move like Ford Pills, so how come there's so much hand-clasping and woeing and frowning at production capacity. One good reason is Ford's outdated, low output Homebush plant where the cars are assembled. Indeed that's no criticism of the Homebush vehicle assemblers — they've been working their hearts out since August — the plant is simply too old and the current industry situation means 'keep the belts tight'.

The Escort is an attempt to introduce new marketing techniques onto the Australian scene. We've covered them before, but to reiterate — instead of offering base models with option availability, the companies now option-up the cars to a certain degree with 'most popular' options and flog the unit at a higher price. Usually the options aren't 'delete' options and you wear the higher cost (albeit with the benefits of better trim and equipment) and the companies carry off the increased profit margins to their friendly bank managers. The logical extension of that premise is the Ford Escort Ghia, which simply abounds in features — what saves it of course is the almost unbelievable pricing and

---

CAPACITIES AND EQUIPMENT

Fuel tank:	40.9 litres
Cooling system:	6.0 litres
Engine sump:	3.8 litres
Battery:	12V 38Ah
Alternator:	28A

CALCULATED DATA

Power to weight:	7.25 kg/kW
Piston speed at max. rpm:	1009 m/min
Specific power output:	81.9 kW/litre

PERFORMANCE

FUEL CONSUMPTION

	Litres/100km	(MPG)
Average for test:	10	28.02
Best recorded:	8.8	31.8
Possible best (under optimum conditions)	8.4	33.5

ACCELERATION

	Manual
0-40km/h	4s
0-60km/h	6.2s
0-80km/h	9.25s
0-100km/h	13.1s
0-110km/h	15.9s
0-120km/h	21.1s
0-130km/h	30.6s

OVERTAKING TIMES

km/h	Drive
40-70	4.8s
50-80	5.9s
60-100	8.9s
80-110	7.1s
100-130	9.8s

STANDING 400M

Average:	19.4s
Best Run:	19.2s

SPEEDS IN GEARS

	Drive	Max. km/h Held	rpm
1st	65	72	5500 (6000)
2nd	112	120	5500 (6000)
3rd	159	159	

BRAKING

Three maximum stops from 50km/h:

Stop	G-force	Pedal Pressure (kg)	Distance (M)
1	1.0g	20	9.4
2	1.0g	22	9.2
3	1.0g	22	9.1

Five maximum stops from 100 km/h:

Stop	G-force	Pedal Pressure (kg)	Distance (M)
1	0.93g	24	42
2	0.89g	22	44.4
3	0.87g	22	44.8
4	0.87g	24	45.0
5	0.87g	24	45.1

---

the fact that it's a bloody nice little car.

The Escort Ghia isn't aimed at any particular sort of buyer, just somebody who wants a bit better trim and equipment level. There isn't anything on the market to touch it and Ford will really score well if it can sort out its supply problems.

The redesign of the Escort, in engineering terms, was wholly successful. The modifications effected by Bahnsen's team have produced a very attractive, practical, wholly conventional and economical small car and it's reasonably good value for money. The increased glass area is great for visibility, but cabin heat buildup is almost incredibly fast and furious. The suspension changes were small, but very effective and the addition of the new C3 automatic transmission is a major factor in the smoothness of the Escort Ghia. The T-bar shifter is now a mechanical linkage, rather than cable-operated, the ride has been smoothed-out and the little car gets a really useful (0.292cu metres) boot. The styling is clean and efficient and general comfort levels have been markedly improved. In fact the Escort Two is *nothing* like its predecessor and the Ghia version sets new standards again.

The handling is precise and very positive. The little car is easy to push around, with the tail becoming a sort of plaything. You need the additional power of the Ghia to have any real fun, but in up-market form the new Escort is a lot sportier than the L/XL models. Now's the time to buy a Ghia manual if you want the ultimate Escort, before the Ford emissions boys hang the single barrel carby on the 1600 engine later this year.

The brakes on the test car were quite good, but there was some rear lock-up and fade during our test stops. The Escort now has the same size front discs as the Cortina and this means very impressive stopping potential for the lighter body.

Fuel consumption on test was quite

GHIA ESCORT

acceptable with an average for the test period of 28 mpg and a best recorded of 31.8 mpg. We believe the careful driver will easily achieve 34 mpg driving a manual car. The auto test car covered the standing 400m in under 20 seconds and overtaking times in Drive were quite consistent.

The Escort Ghia is a nice piece of motor car design for the people who want a bit more and are prepared to pay for it. The pricing is attractive and the overall package is well-planned.

The service intervals are listed as every 10,000km and the mechanicals are straightforward and easy to work on. We see no reason why the Escort should not be an extremely economical and practical car to own and operate. So Ford, it's all up to you. ⓗ

(Continued from page 98)

Then coil-spring damper units using all racing car components were fitted. They are mounted vertically to the body off their own mounting brackets welded to the axle housing. Armstrong adjustable shockers are fitted.

A "monoplate" dummy spring of mild spring steel was then "pinned" to the axle housing and attached to the regular leaf spring mounts to "simulate" the standard suspension — which was necessary to comply with regulations. It does no work, and in fact, will be removed for 1972 racing which doesn't require it.

Final touches to the rear end were the installation of 9¼in. disc brakes and the fitting of a Hewland limited slip differential to the housing.

At the front end, all locating points were moved to suit lowering and new suspension geometry. In the engine compartment, the extensions for the McPherson strut top mounts are clearly evident — this has the effect of lowering the suspension but retaining the same amount of vertical travel.

The struts themselves were completely modified — the coils thrown away and replaced with tiny 2½in. diameter racing car springs and the base mounting plate modified accordingly. Adjustable Konis were fitted.

A lower diagonal rear link was added each side to locate the struts — and the roll bar now no longer acts as a locating unit, leaving it free to perform its proper function.

ESCORTS FOR RACE & RALLY

(Continued from page 98)

to allow the electrical system to be "killed" without removing battery connections, there are two coils mounted under the bonnet so the leads can be quickly transferred in a failure, two complete regulators bolted under the dash, so the navigator can unclip the master plug and switch across if one system fails, and big indexed fuse boxes.

Special switches on the dash provide flood lighting for the bonnet, boot and rear seat area, left tank/right tank gauge reading (with master fuel flow switch on the floor between the seats), plus separate high beam master switches to allow the navigator to grab full beam independent of the driver.

There are also lights for reversing, red rear (emergency stops etc), and navigaotor's reading light (normal Butler lamp). Each has its own warning light to avoid being left on accidentally.

The lighting system itself is a major work of art. The headlights contain two 55 watt Cibie Biodes each — and it was quickly discovered the intense heat these generated melted the little rubber mounting plug for the parking light inside the headlamp and spread yellow sulphur over the lens.

Cibie's John Holsworth flew-out special plastic heat-resistant plugs from France, which cured the problem — but the parkers had to be moved down onto the bodywork and a separate circuit created.

COST SCHEDULE

Make/Model: . . . . Ford Escort
Ghia Auto
Pricing: $4793
Registration: $120
Insurance Category: 3
Rates quoted below are for drivers over 25 with 60 percent no-claim bonus and where the car is under hire-purchase. This is the minimum premium level — decreasing rates of experience and lower age groups may have varying excesses and possible premium loadings.
Non-tariff: $153.60
Tariff: $180.00
N.R.M.A. $169.55

Warranty: 12 mths/20,000km

Service:
Initial service is free. This covers the first

1500km and includes lubrication and maintenance (materials chargeable).

Other Services:
Lubrication and maintenance services at 3000km, 5000km, 10,000km and every 10,000km thereafter.

Spare Parts:
(Recommended cost breakdown)
Disc Pads (set of four) $17.60
Muffler (Front) $35.00
Muffler (Rear) $25.00
Windscreen . . . . . $35.20 (Armour plate)
$85 (Laminated)
Shock Absorbers: Front $66.47
Rear $36.00
Headlamp Assembly $35.40
Taillamp Assembly $35.70
Bumpers: Front $30.50
Rear $30.50
Front Guard: $48.50

Rose-joints were used throughout and a spherical bearing replaced the normal rubber bush in the steering arm location. The standard rack was retained because of the extortionate cost of a magnesium rack.

Front and rear ends are fully set-up for adjustable ride height, and complete wheel balancing was done on a set of scales — just like a racing car.

Spring rates were chosen after extensive track test sessions with at least 50 different types of springs until the right balance was achieved. It is basically hard front, soft rear for initial understeer progressing to gentle roll-oversteer.

All hubs were fitted with specially machined extended mounting bolts to take the fat 10in. wide Lolita-type CAC-cast magnesium 13in. wheels — fitted up with Goodyear G23 rubber sized at 475/1085 x 13 all round.

Then came the vital powerplant. Fanning bought a stock retail Twin Cam block "across the counter" and the crew set to work with routine all-steel mods, special pistons etc.

They then tacked-on a BRM twin-cam head with quite a distinguished history — it has had eight years of continued full racing use, dating back to original equipment on BRM works cars, and eventually Allan Moffatt's TransAm Lotus Cortina (the gearbox also came from this car).

It was fitted-up with Vegantune/Lucas injection equipment — basically Lucas gear, with special machine work by Vegantune.

However, Hindmarsh made up his

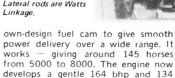

PEEK-A-BOO at rear end shows some of the suspension secrets that have put the car on top. Lateral rods are Watts Linkage.

own-design fuel cam to give smooth power delivery over a wide range. It works — giving around 145 horses from 5000 to 8000. The engine now develops a gentle 164 bhp and 134 lbs.ft of torque.

The final modification was dry-sumping — the reservoir, pumps and filters are located in the boot for better weight distribution.

The transmission was put together 12 months ago and hasn't been touched. It is naturally equipped with a close-ratio set, and is usually matched to a 4.7 final — only Surfers Paradise demands a 4.1 tail.

It's joined to the engine via a magnesium bell-housing — the only concession to weight-saving in this area.

Not surprisingly there's immense detail work. The brakes have adjustable balance bar to control rear-end effort and the separate-circuit rear brakes are further controlled with a smaller master cylinder.

In fitting up the mechanical equipment, any non-body part was drilled for lightness (without sacrificing strength) — even down to the brake pedal arm. The heater came out of course.

The ultimate result is a car that weighs a little over 1600lbs ready to race with a magnificent 55/45 front/rear weight balance.

It took 640 man-hours to put together initially, and apart from suspension sorting (spring/damper rates, etc) it's had no major additional work in 12 highly successful months of racing.

The car has finished in all except one event and it has had only one (minor) engine rebuild, no transmission maintenance and no other mechanical work apart from detail race preparation.

But early in the New Year it takes a giant step forward to keep abreast of changing rules. Bill Fanning has decided to go for Sports Closed competition because many circuits will mix Improved Tourers and Sports Closed tourers in all races.

The Fanning Formula for 1972 race success is an 1864 cc Waggott FVA, (an extra 80/90 bhp) a five-speed gearbox, four-piston McLaren ventilated discs and some appropriate suspension tweaks

Right now he should be beating a dozen sponsors from the door! Make way for "Easy Rider". ■

ESCORTS FOR RACE & RALLY

The auxiliary lighting comes from two 100 watt 11 in. Cibie Oscars mounted in the centre and two 55 watt 9 in. Oscars on the outside pointing sideways for corner diffusion.

The big 55 amp Bosch alternator is right on the limit of its capacity powering this system, but it has proved completely reliable. A big heavy duty battery is bolted in a special steel case in the boot and is guaranteed to stay intact — even upside down!

The rest of the preparation was sheer detail work — items like a massive sump guard that extends to the transmission, suspension tuning (1 deg negative is all the front end is set-up with), fitting full aircraft style harness for the driver, and more rudimentary one for the navigator to give him more free movement, windscreen washers on the blades with big one-gallon reservoir in the cockpit and powerful Japanese electric pump, fitting Halda Twinmaster and clock, bolting-in spare tyres, warning triangles, axe and shovel, and hundreds of tiny details.

Finally, the road gear got special attention. Inglis started with Veith rubber which he ran for one rally before swapping to Uniroyals — which he has stuck with ever since.

He uses 175HR Uniroyal 240s almost exclusively — although he has tried the regular Winterides for certian mud conditions in special rally stages. Normal pressures are 30 psi all-round,

INGLIS is well-belted in with aircraft harness behind Ford works wheel ready to tackle toughest rally sections in comfort.

though for Rallycross 36 front 30 rear was necessary for the big jumps.

The engine is healthy — but remains very close to standard. Bob started running it virtually completely standard, then tried works L1 camshafts for the Dulux.

These gave about 140 bhp, but narrowed the usable rev range, and he has since switched to a 30/60 D-Type grind, which pulls 126 bhp at 6500 and 116 lbs. ft. of torque at 4000 on the Town and Country Dyno.

In that condition, the engine has now done 10,000 hard rally miles since its last rebuild — and most of that time it has been operating at around 6500. Bob trusts the engine, because he knows it is tough and reliable — but he has a different attitude to all the other

components. Brakes, bearings, diff, gearbox, suspension, linkages etc. are constantly checked and replaced — as often as once a rally.

And that is why the car has never let him down. With a combination of reliability, and complete tightness, he knows instantly if anything is wrong.

The car has given him a Southern Cross eleventh, Dulux ninth and more recently, Hill Rally eleventh — good placings for a private car — and helped pull in "Father Christmas" in the shape of sponsor John Hile Ford who is a dedicated follower of the car and the sport.

The car has now had one season of full-blooded competition, and it's just getting into gear. You're sure to hear more and better things in 1972. ■

Ford's Racy RS 2000 For Australia . . . .

THE ULTIMATE

ESCORT

FORD AUSTRALIA will release a limited number of the sporty RS 2000 Escorts onto the Australian market for restricted sale. The RS 2000 is the hottest version of the new 'Brenda' Escort to come here. The RS 2000 has a top speed of 180km/h and races to 100km/h from rest in just under 9.5 secs.

The car is distinguished by a foam-filled plastic 'snout' with quad headlights, 5.5 lightweight cast wheels and a rear spoiler. The 2000cc engine is a SOHC unit linked to Ford's excellent single-rail four-speed manual transmission and returns around 28 mpg under touring conditions. Ford Australia is anxious to introduce the RS 2000 as soon as possible in order to arrange homologation with Australian motor sport regulations as laid down by C.A.M.S.

Although the company officially withdrew from direct participation in

From
'DEV' DVORETSKY
in London

motor sport it's well known that the marketing division has been laying in some heavy pressure to support the competition activities of private entrants. The RS 2000 could be the company's rally hopeful and could be an interesting class entrant in the Hardie Ferodo 1000 at Bathurst, where it would do battle with the two-litre BMW, Alfa and Dolomite Sprint.

It's not yet known how many of these red-hot Escorts Ford plans to import, but the first shipment of 25 cars has already been organised and it's hoped they will arrive in mid-March. Ford was planning to display an RS 2000 at the Melbourne Motor Show had they arrived in time, but latest information says that when the RS 2000s do land in Australia they will be assigned to picked dealer

outlets and sale of cars generally will be aimed at competition drivers first up. Although it's not really a devastating machine the RS 2000 has nonetheless won a reputation as a tight, taut touring car with good road manners and lots of flair.

The Escort RS 2000 has to be my nomination, however, for the greatest bit of fun-car Ford (or perhaps anyone) has yet come up with. By fun I don't mean boy racer, hanging the back out on every corner and making enough din to attract every cop the neighbourhood! I mean fun because it's safe, handles like only sports cars were once supposed to, and goes like the proverbial ding-bats road-runner — only faster! Yet it can potter around the main street and not splutter and tutter and generally drive everyone mad. It's not a rally car (though its looks and top speed of 184 km/h may belie the fact) but you can rush it around all week doing a lot of high

MODERN MOTOR — MAY 1976

speed running and tough, tyre-screeching acceleration runs, and at the end the motor is still singing happily right in tune.

The refined two-litre belt-driven ohc was originally used in Pinto and Cortina. Now Ford has managed, with the help of a new exhaust manifold and different exhaust system, to extract a bit more to bring it from 73 kW (DIN) at 5500 rpm, as it used to be, to 82 kW at the same revs.

The motor has been coupled via a new sound-deadening lightweight alloy bell housing to the excellent four-speed Cortina single-rail gearbox, and the gear-lever has been cut to stubby proportions, which makes cog-swapping an absolute delight. There's a bit of a gap in the ratios between first and second, but the rest are nigh on perfect. With a final drive ratio of 3.45:1 the gearing gives 30 km/h per thousand rpm in top gear. Combine that with the extra torque — up from 150 Nm at 3500 rpm to 161 Nm at 4000 rpm — and you have a very flexible, long-legged little road eater that won't disgrace any carport!

Apart from a little low-speed boom it's quiet inside and out and has the most impeccable manners. The quietness comes from increased soundproofing and the use of that alloy bell-housing. The extra manners come from somewhat stiffer spring rates and twin trailing arms replacing the former anti-roll bar on the leaf-spring rear axle, and slightly different front-end geometry.

It proves the point I've often made — a well located live rear end is as good as most independents. Ford

"A real good looker that won't disgrace any carport" — that's the RS 2000 which is visually attractive but keeps practicality in mind.

aimed at a compromise between soft ride and better handling, and achieved it. I'll put up with a bit of radial bump-thump from the CN36 Pirelli 175/70 tyres when the car is taken over the rough.

The RS 2000 is the sort of car that mum or dad can use with equal happiness. He will love the slick-shifting gearbox, the beautifully direct steering, the acceleration (0-100 km/h in 8.5 sec) and high (up to 140-plus km/h) cruising speed. Mum will have no complaints locking junior in the rear seat and putting plenty of shopping in the boot. She may complain the steering is a bit heavy at low speeds but it's lighter than some less potent six and eight cylinder jobs she's used to driving in Australia.

What she will love is the down to 40 km/h and under top gear flexibility, the all-round visibility, and the well-finished black interior with its cloth rally-type front seats.

The sloping black plastic grille front, with the quad Cibie headlight treatment and bumper-height broad black side stripe make it a real good-looker. The front under-bumper spoiler does make a difference to roadholding though I still have my doubts of that black rubber one bolted to the boot!

These rally-type seats occupy a bit more space than usual and cut off rear seat leg-room to some extent, but they offer tremendous support (though they are inclined to raise the thighs unusually high at first). The

RS 2000 is, like all Fords in Europe these days, very well equipped, with door-pull armrests, dual sun visors (which will only face front and can't be twisted to cut out sideways sun glare!) and built-in headrests.

The black dashboard is well laid out with a neat cubby hole for smokes and the like on the left and a neat instrument cluster in front of the driver on the right (there is, of course, a fair sized glove box on the passenger side). The instrument cluster is the standard pattern for Ford these days — two big round dials for tacho and speedo with trip, surrounded by three smaller gauges for fuel, volts and water temperature. Five warning lights beneath the three smaller dials completes the neat layout.

I give a big black mark to Ford Germany which now builds the RS 2000 at Saarlouis) for not switching the steering column stalk controls from one side to the other when it swapped the steering wheel from LHD to RHD. There should be a law everywhere making it illegal not to have the indicator stalk (which usually doubles as a headlight flasher warning device) on the side *away* from the gear lever!

The fuel tank, of only 40-litres, is another bad point. While the RS 2000 trounces all its opposition (the Alfetta GTs, BMW 320s, Celica GTs, Audi 80 GTs, and Lancia Betas) in the performance bracket, it doesn't come out so well in consumption. It's not bad, but it's certainly not good. Gentle pottering over long distances might return 30 mpg, but spirited driving, tramping through the second choke of the excellent

THE OVERHEAD camshaft motor fits snugly into the engine bay providing reasonable accessibility.

Weber carb, will smartly increase consumption to 24 mpg or worse. That puts a maximum range of little more than 400 km at best and 300/350 km more likely.

Speaking of the competition, about the only thing that will live with the RS 2000 is the Dolomite Sprint, which you should be getting used to by now. Apart from the Sprint none of the cars I've mentioned can match the RS 2000 up to 100 km/h.

While top speed of 177 km/h (and you can cruise all day on the right road at 145 km/h) can be bettered by the Alfetta, Toyota and Sprint, all — in Europe anyway — are in a price bracket above the Ford.

Only the BMW 320 and Sprint might claim to be perhaps a little better finished and perhaps a bit quieter though even that would be in doubt. Get moving on the open road, in most conditions, and the Escort

RS 2000 comes out well. It handles as well as any, is less fussy than most (particularly the lower capacity cars) and has just as long legs (apart from the fuel capacity).

The brakes I'm not sure of. After seven days of driving in frosty weather with the car left outside all night, I wondered what some of my colleagues running around at the same time in similar models were complaining about. But on my way back to Ford's Chiswick test-car hide-away one frosty morning, a bloke in a Honda four Bog-wheeler (cor, in weather like that!) almost went under me. I slapped on the disc front, drum rear, anchors to find the rears had locked — and I was pulling towards the kerb. Still, I did try to repeat the effort (in a quiet cul-de-sac) but couldn't get them to pull anything but straight. Even the rears didn't seem to lock up so much. Can only imagine it might have been

a bit of rust or damp on the discs or the pads. Incidentally, despite the icy conditions, the automatic choke helped start the car first turn every time!

The RS 2000 costs $A3905 basic in UK, just 75 per cent more than the Escort 1300 L model, which in Australia sells for $A3516 — about 60 percent more than in UK ex-factory.

Old model RS 2000s sold for about $6500, so with inflation and other rising costs we can expect the new model RS 2000 to pricetag at about $7000-$7500. At that price it will challenge all those in its (European) class — the Alfetta GT, the yet-to-arrive BMW 320, and the Celica Sprint. Only the Celica would be below it. Drop round to your local Ford man and ask him to let you have a look when they do get Down Under. ⒽⒽ

ROAD TEST DATA & SPECIFICATIONS

Manufacturer: ...Ford Motor Co. Saarlouis
Make/Model: ...Escort RS2000
Body type: ...2-door sedan
Test car supplied by: ...Ford Motor Co., Warley, Essex England

ENGINE
Location: ...Front
Cylinders: ...4 in-line
Bore & Stroke: ...90.82 x 76.95mm
Capacity: ...1993cc
Compression: ...9.2 to 1
Aspiration: ...Weber 2V downdraft carburettor
Fuel pump: ...Mechanical
Valve gear: ...SOHC
Maximum power: ...82kW @ 5500rpm
Maximum torque: ...160 Nm @ 4000rpm

TRANSMISSION
Type/locations: ...4-speed manual
Driving wheels: ...rear
Clutch type: ...sdp

Gear	Gearbox ratios
1st	3.65
2nd	1.97
3rd	1.37
4th	1.00
Final drive:	3.54:1

SUSPENSION
Front suspension: ...Macpherson strut, coil springs telescopic dampers, anti-roll bar
Rear suspension: ...Live, radius arms and semi-elliptic leaf springs
Shock absorbers: ...Direct-acting telescopic
Wheels: ...Cast light alloy 6J x 13
Tyres: ...Pirelli CN36 175/70 HR-13

STEERING
Type: ...Rack and pinion
Turns lock to lock: ...3.5
Wheel diameter: ...380mm
Turning circle: ...9.7m

BRAKES
Front: ...Disc — Diameter: 243mm
Rear: ...Drum — Diameter: 228mm
Servo assistance: ...Vacuum standard

DIMENSIONS AND WEIGHT
Wheelbase: ...2403mm
Overall length: ...4140mm
width: ...1600mm
height: ...1385mm
Track, front: ...1289mm
rear: ...1315mm
Ground clearance: ...260mm
Kerb weight: ...941kg

CAPACITIES AND EQUIPMENT
Fuel tank: ...40.86 litres
Cooling system: ...6.81 litres
Engine sump: ...3.74 litres
Battery: ...12 v 57 Ah
Alternator: ...45 amp, 220/120 watt

PERFORMANCE

FUEL CONSUMPTION

	Litres/100km	(MPG)
Average for test:	12.73	22.1
Best recorded:	11.28	25
Possible best (under optimum conditions):	9.4	30

ACCELERATION

	Manual
0-40km/h	2.2s
0-60km/h	4.0s
0-80km/h	6.0s
0-100km/h	9.0s
0-110km/h	11.2s
0-120km/h	13.0s
0-130km/h	16.0s

OVERTAKING TIMES (holding gears)

km/h	3rd	4th
40-70	7s	9s
50-80	5s	7.5s
60-100	6s	8.0s
80-100	5s	8.2s
100-130		13.0s

STANDING

400m:	16.8s

SPEED IN GEARS

	Max. km/h	rpm
1st	55	6600
2nd	100	6600
3rd	145	6600
4th	184	6000

FORD'S RS SPECIALS

BASICALLY it's just a two-door Escort sedan — but a close look at this cutaway reveals lots of goodies which are far from standard. Check the four-wheel discs, DOHC Hart-Ford engine, roll-cage and modified rear suspension.

Ford's Escort-based RS series is leading the company right into a boots 'n' all rally effort that is taking it to the top of the ladder – fast. With a contingent of the giant –killing RS 1800s entered for the Southern Cross we decided to take a look under the skin and find out why these bright rising stars are so good . . .

SINCE Ford first imported a limited number of RS2000 Escorts into Australia there has been speculation that they would be backing motorsport again. The new European look Escort is a real success story already and the addition of the RS2000 version adds further to the range but only to a very select group of Australian enthusiasts.

But this car is only the 'tip of the iceberg' of the Escort range of goodies available to enthusiasts in England. We had the opportunity recently to see the behind the scenes activities of Ford's competition department in England and road test the ultimate production line RS1800 Escort.

Added interest follows Ford's announcement that they will be entering two UK works prepared RS1800 Escorts in the coming Southern Cross Rally at Port Macquarie NSW. Drivers will be Roger Clark and Timo Makinen, two of

MODERN MOTOR, NOVEMBER, 1976

the quickest and most experienced rally drivers in the world today.

The team will be backed up by mechanics, team mangers and loads of spares all from England. Ford Australia will also assist with service crews and preparation.

Escorts currently dominate the rally scene in the UK but here in Australia with no factory participation they are rarely seen in major events against the many Datsuns and Lancers. However this may change having seen the meticulous preparation the works Escort's are currently going through at Boreham.

The Group 2 rally Escort RS1800 is basically the same as the regular production Escort RS1800 although the Group 2 rally car incorporates modifications and refinements to cope with the extraordinary demands of international rallying.

Under-body protection is increased by

the addition of a light weight alloy shield which covers the underside of the engine and gearbox. The twin overhead camshaft 1800cc, 16-valve, 4-cylinder engine has its capacity increased to 2-litres and with the addition of two twin choke 45mm Weber carburettors — replacing the single twin choke, down draught Weber — with modified camshafts engine power output is increased to an average 171.5kW at 8,200 rpm.

Brian Hart prepares and tunes all the works engines and power goes to 183kW on some engines. Additionally, the engine's lubrication system is changed to the dry sump type with the oil reservoir located in the boot of the Escort.

The four-speed gearbox is changed to a ZF five speed and a limited slip differential is incorporated in the rear axle. In order to produce high rates of acceleration with a comparatively low maximum

speed the ratio of the final drive unit is also changed between a 5.1 or 5.3.

Last year no less than 8 different types of Dunlop tyres ranging from extra wide, hand-cut racing tyres to narrow snow tyres were available to the drivers in the Ford 'works' team. The Minilite alloy, extra wide wheels are enclosed within special wheelarch extensions and both the front and rear suspensions systems incorporate gas/oil filled Bilstein shock absorber units.

Rear axle location is also improved and modified by the addition of extra suspension links. In order to provide maximum protection for the occupants of the rally Escort RS1800 a special steel safety cage is built into the car and mounted to the body at 14 points.

Full aircraft type seat harnesses are provided for both driver and navigator, a special fireproof bulkhead is built across the rear of the car between the boot and

Motorsport

the passenger compartment, and the long range fuel tank which is mounted in the boot is filled with plastic foam to prevent fuel spillage in the event of the tank being ruptured.

All fuel and brake lines are routed through the inside of the car for protection while the front and rear brake systems are on separate circuits.

The ignition can be switched off from either inside or outside the car and a special fire extinguishing system is fitted. In case of fire the system automatically releases a special gas which extinguishes the flames but is not dangerous to the occupants of the car.

The international rallies have formed a particularly important part of Ford's Escort development programmes. The many improvements which have been brought about in suspension, brakes, lights, comfort and durability in today's production car have been developed in competition. Additionally, the specialist components which are fitted to Ford 'works' rally cars are available to the private owner who wishes to compete in competition.

Ford performance parts are marketed throughout Britain and Europe through the network of Ford Rallye Sport Dealers. The Ford Rallye Sport Club concentrates more and more on providing technical information for its members who wish to take part in motor sport competition.

A series of facts sheets which can be incorporated into a comprehensive binder to make up a complete volume on rally preparation is distributed to members. This new facts service is designed to enable the private entrant to keep pace with the works drivers.

As a further part of its activity, the Ford Rallye Sport Club has established a comprehensive film library of motor sport films. These include the 1973 Scottish, the 1972 Safari and the Ford instructional film on rally driving. New additions to the library include the filmed report of the 1975 Lombard-RAC rally and the 1975 Scottish.

With an annual turnover now exceeding $30,000 and almost half of it going for export, the Ford Rallye Sport Club's clothing range now extends from Timo's Lombard-RAC rally winning hat to marshalls' golf-style umbrellas. The range of clothing also includes light, medium and heavyweight jackets, T-shirts, key rings and badges.

MODERN MOTOR, NOVEMBER, 1976

All this gives you an idea as to how enthusiastically Ford follow up their motorsport involvement. What hope for Australian Ford enthusiasts? Lets wait until after the Southern Cross rally!

DRIVING IMPRESSIONS

WE COLLECTED the RS1800 Escort from Ford's head office at Brentwood in Essex, and headed straight for Boreham where the work's cars are prepared and serviced. The standard road going RS1800 not only has good under the bonnet performance but it handled like a sports car. Very tight, smooth with the comfort of a touring car.

Imported from Germany the overall finish was excellent with full bucket contour seats and cloth trim.

The original engine began as a Cosworth FVA enlarged from 1600 to 1800cc using an aluminium block and head housing four valves per cylinder. The current capacity is 1854cc with a 10.1 compression ratio and 93kW at 6500 rpm plus 162 Nm torque at 4000 rpm.

We were expecting racing type engine characteristics, rough idle, hard to start and not working under 5000 revs. How wrong we were! The new engine uses a single twin choke Weber which provided easy starts, extreme flexibility even in London's peak hour traffic. Putting the foot down in top gear at 60 km/h gives smooth fuss-free acceleration.

The works rally Escorts run a 5 speed gear box but the road going RS1800 has a smooth shifting 4 speed. A standard 3.54 differential unit is used instead of an

LSD. This proved quite satisfactory for city and highway driving. Top gear performance was extremely flexible, pulling from 1500 rpm, most uncharacteristic for a race bred engine.

We drove the Escort RS1800 over 1100 km which included a one day trip up the M1 freeway from London to Leeds, across to North Wales then through the tight twisting mountain roads of Wales down to Cardiff and to Bristol. Arriving back in London in time for peak hour traffic jams.

Throughout the trip the BDA engine ran quietly cruising at 112 km/h and showed 4300 rpm at 128 km/h with rapid acceleration right up to 190 km/h. Even with the single twin-choke Weber the Escort will reach 0-95 km/h in 8.6 seconds but using all gears to the limit helps, as over 3500 rpm there was a definite surge of power.

A performance car like the RS1800 tempts one to use the gears far more frequently, reving it out to 6500 and driving it like a sports car. Even driven hard the BDA return 25mpg.

Roadholding throughout the tight Welsh mountain roads was excellent. Ford's involvement in competition has paid off with this road machine. Suspension is very similar to works rally RS1800 we saw inside Boreham.

The live rear axle had additional radius arms and heavier leaf springs with Bilstein gas shockers all combining to stop any rear axle movement. Up front the McPherson struts are again Bilsteins, heavy duty springs and anti roll bar.

The ride is firm and sure, no body roll or rear axle hop, just complete contact

LOOKING deceptively domestic the RS 1800 is a real Q-car. Minimal exterior jazz-up hides 171kW engine and five-speed gearbox which gives the little car a top speed of 185km/h and acceleration of 6.9seconds from zero to 100km/h.

*M*otorsport

with the bitumen at all times. Completely predictable with power at your foot to give some added on-off cornering assistance. Unfortunately time did not allow us the opportunity to try out the RS1800 on the dirt, but from all reports, it is just as responsive.

Interior layout was well designed with tachometer and speedo clearly layed out directly in front of the neat vinyl padded wheel, along with an oil pressure temp and fuel gauge clearly marked white on black. Driver comfort rates very highly with excellent contoured hip hugging fabric covered seats.

Visibility was excellent, and a 12 hour trip in the Escort proved that the seats really work.

So how much does this ultimate little sports sedan cost, in UK you pay $4905 for the standard version or with extra door trimmings, reclining seats, head restraints, inertia seat belts, carpeted boot, centre console and glove box, it costs $5118.

So what price here in Australia? We don't like to guess but if ever the little tourer comes out here, you'll have to stand in line. ∎

FORD ESCORT RS1800 SPECIFICATION

BASIC VEHICLE:
Escort RS1800, 2-door, 4-seater saloon of unitary steel construction. In rally form the car has a top speed in excess of 115 mph/185 km/h, and accelerates from 0 to 60 mph/96.5 km/h in under 7 seconds.

Engine
(Alloy block, 4-cylinder in-line, water-cooled)
Bore..90.00 mm
Stroke..77.7 mm
Cubic capacity...1,977cc
Compression ratio ....11.5 : 1
Power output ....171kW at 8,200 rpm
Maximum torque ....226 Nm
Maximum engine speed..............................8,500 rpm
Fuel supply.....................Twin 45 DCOE or 48 DCOE
                                              Weber carburettors

Gearbox
(ZF, five forward synchronised ratios)
First..2.3 : 1
Second...1.8 : 1
Third...1.36 : 1
Fourth...1.14 : 1
Fifth...1.0 : 1
Rear axle ratio..5.3/5.1 : 1

Brakes:
Front, 241 mm diameter ventilated discs; rear, 254 mm diameter solid discs with twin calipers; twin brake servos.

Wheels:
Alloy 13 ins diameter, rim widths 5, 6, 7 or 8 ins, Dunlop competition tyres.

Shock absorbers:
Bilstein gas-filled.

Steering:
Rack and pinion, geared 2½ turns lock to lock. Sports steering wheel with leather rim.

Lights:
Cibie head and auxiliary lamps with quartz halogen bulbs.

THE INTERIOR of Roger Clark's car shows masses of rally aids screwed onto a standard Escort dashboard. Makinen's car is much more complicated, with a great deal more equipment.

THIS is the shell of Roger's car for Australia's Southern Cross rally. The body is specially stiffened with additional welding and the rear suspension is modified.

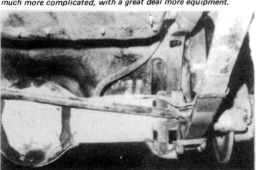

AT THE rear there's additional links to tighten axle location. Note Panhard bar and disc brake. Ahead of the axle there's radius rods and alloy plates to protect the differential.

THE BDA 2000cc engine for Roger Clark's car — it's prepared by tuner Brian Hart, one of Britain's top engine specialist, and produces 183kW (245bhp).

MODERN MOTOR, NOVEMBER, 1976

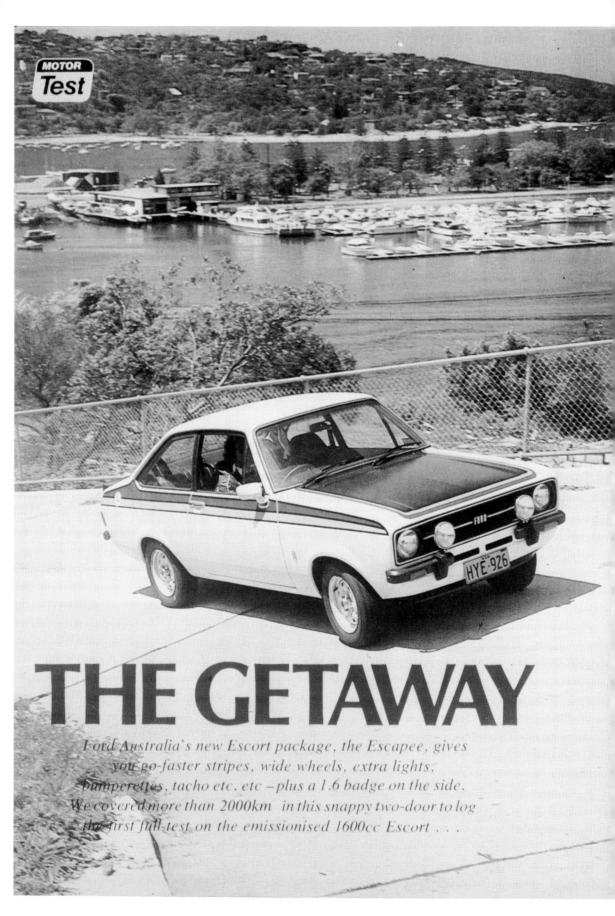

THE GETAWAY

*Ford Australia's new Escort package, the Escapee, gives
you go-faster stripes, wide wheels, extra lights,
bumperettes, tacho etc. etc – plus a 1.6 badge on the side.
We covered more than 2000km in this snappy two-door to log
the first full-test on the emissionised 1600cc Escort . . .*

Escort 1.6L 2-door	Report: John Crawford

IT DOESN'T really matter whether Ford's Escort is a good car, or a bad car, it will sell almost regardless. How many it sells is the critical question.

Back in September of 1975 Ford Australia realised it would at last be able to get serious about competing with the Japanese small light cars. The then-current Escort was a reasonable performer in that area of the market, but compared with the dynamite performance of the Toyota Corolla and the Datsun 1200/120Y it was a hopeless flop.

Ford launched the facelifted Escort (codenamed Brenda) onto an even more competitive market. It had been beaten to the punch by arch rival GM-H which had introduced the zippy little Gemini in March and the car had received a great reception both from the motoring press and the public.

By the time Ford's baby bowed things had really hotted-up. In an effort to knock Corolla off the top perch GM-H was really hitting car buyers between the eyes with Gemini promotion.

Ford's first predictions for the fiercely contested small/light segment was 16,000 units — or 15.5 to 16 percent of the market.

By the end of 1976, just over a year after introduction, about 14,400 Escorts will have been sold, representing 12.8 percent of the small/light sector. FoMoCo predicts sales will run to about 15,200 in 1977.

Obviously the battle is hot, but Escort has proved very popular in the market place. Launched with overtones of a European heritage the first few months of sale proved a headache for Ford marketing men.

Based on the performance and model mix of the superseded car Ford programmed far too many two-door models in the first batch. The four-door and Ghia sales outstripped even its most conservative estimates. Production programming was modified and now the four-door XL Escort is the best-selling version in the range (6261 vs. 4488).

This car lines up against formidable opposition, both in terms of design, equipment, size and price — not to mention performance, and in the first

months of sale Ford dealers would rather not have mentioned performance.

The company decided to retain the 1300cc engine for the new Escort. In retrospect this may have been a wise decision, but many people criticised the action and prayed for the day Ford Australia would see the error of its ways and bump the base engine up to 1600. However much people defend the old 1300 (and it wasn't all that bad) there's no doubt the Escort is a much better car for the extra 300cc capacity.

Sales have been so strong that it's been difficult to get hold of a 1600 for test, so when Ford released the special 'Escapee' package (coincidentally at the same time as the Southern Cross Rally) we decided it was time to put Ford's little baby against its competition, and the stopwatch.

The Escapee is all bolt-on gear and pretty striping — mechanically it's identical to the rest of the range, but sporty to look at and it proved fun to drive.

DESIGN

THE TEAM of German designers at Ford's Cologne Research Centre, under Uwe Bahnsen, did a very clever piece of salvaging when they executed the 'Brenda' restyle program. Retaining the floorpan, firewall and most inner skins they simply drew up a new set of outer skins and a new cabin design.

In effect the new Escort is quite an efficient and economical facelift, but the end result is a body with excellent visibility, strong visual appeal and a reasonably timeless shape which is clean and aerodynamically streamlined.

Drag factors played an important part in determining the shape of the small bib

spoiler integrated into the sheet metal under the grille.

There were very marginal increases in interior dimensions and some change to exterior packaging, but essentially the new Escort is identical in size to its predecessor. The boot is a useful size, but fuel tank capacity is miserably small. It's not really a car for four adults, but they can be accommodated over short distances.

The body you see now will hold until the next, all-new Escort-sized car comes along (around 1979-80) and it will be a front wheel drive package based closely on the Fiesta minicar. In Europe the Escort is sold with 1100cc, 1300cc and 1600cc engines, but for simplicity and compliance with ADR27a we see only one engine in Australia.

POWERTRAIN

I THINK Ford Australia might now be wishing that it *had* introduced the 1600cc powerplant as the Escort base engine at initial release time, as there is definite evidence Escort lost ground in the first months due to Gemini's 1600cc engine and agressive marketing of the Isuzu car by GM-H. However, looking at the Isuzu/Ford 1600cc engines following the introduction of emission rule ADR27a maybe Ford did the right thing after all.

The 1600xx engine fitted to Escort Ghia (pre-27a) used a two-barrell Weber carburettor, but since July first both L, XL and Ghia versions all use the same single (Ford) carburettor 1600cc engine and power is down somewhat. From a marketing sense it was far better to offer a 1600 over a 1300 (after July 1), rather than go to a lower-powered 1600 — which would have been the case had the 2V 1600 been offered from start of production.

Maximum power is developed at 5000rpm, but the engine winds up easily to over 6000 — which can be a trap, because the tacho reads to 7000 and there's no redline. The Kent engine in itself is pretty noisy, but well-designed damping (which is carefully placed in the engine compartment) has almost completely reduced noise transmission to the cabin.

With maximum torque coming in at 2500rpm the engine is quite flexible, and quite surprisingly it will pull without fuss from just under 2000rpm in fourth gear.

The lack of power which shows up in a direct comparison with some of Escort's competitor's isn't really a major concern. As it stands the current Escort offers adequate power and reasonable performance. Mind you, a well run-in 1300cc Escort went pretty well, until you really put the small capacity engine to the test, under full load conditions, so the performance offered by the new single carburettor 1600 is quite sufficient. The crossflow head breathes well despite the lack of previously-fitted, exhaust extractors which gave 'Brenda' a sporty burble under hard acceleration.

Also, with the emphasis on flexibility and reliability there is a natural gain in the fuel consumption department. The 1300 would return figures in excess of 38mpg, driven carefully. We believe the 1600 will run to 37mpg under optimum conditions.

Gearing is an important part of the current 1600's performance package and the ratios are carefully chosen. First is quite low, which gives good initial acceleration, and although there's a decent gap to second you don't really notice it as the little car gets under way quite easily.

The ratio spread between second and top suits engine output characteristics

and makes for good city performance, and acceptable cruising capabilities, even in hilly terrain.

The rear axle ratio is a tallish 3.54 to 1 and at about top whack in fourth gear this gives the little Escort almost 150km/h maximum speed. However at higher cruising speeds we noticed a lot of transmission noise, both in our two-door test car and our LFT van. Maybe the noise is quite normal and the cars need a bit more insulation.

The single diaphragm clutch is light and definitely designed with women in mind. Its take-up is progressive and easy to get used to.

UNDERBODY

THIS STORY has been told before, in descriptions of the previous model. There is little change in suspension settings or layout. The rear shock absrober angles have been altered and anti-roll bars are fitted to some versions, but essentially it's still the same simple McPherson strut front end with semi ellipticals and live rear axle down the back.

Spring and shock absorber rates were altered for Australian conditions, but apart from that there is no change. Back axle location is poor on rough surfaces, but as a town car this does not seem to be a problem.

The rear springs were made wider and the number of leaves were reduced — this, plus lower profile radial ply tyres, has lowered the ride height marginally.

Spring travel is the same, however more progressive bump rubbers were fitted to give improved isolation from suspension noise.

The underbody sheet metal is the same as before, but what mods that were effected have increased structural rigidity and made the whole body stiffer, and subsequently quieter.

The brakes are a power-assisted disc/drum system with healthy 244mm diameter discs to give effective stopping under all conditions. The back brakes locked-up occasionally (with one person on board) and the back end hops around under heavy braking on broken surfaces, but generally we have no complaint with the anchors. Pad life should be greater, due to an increase of 30 percent in pad area.

INTERIOR

THE REAL improvement here is in trim and equipment levels. The subject of this test starts life as a basic L version and gets some dress-up gear, which excludes the heated rear screen and a few other small items.

Basically however Ford has ensured its Escort range matches up with anything the Japanese can offer. There is a price penalty of course, but

ESCAPEE gets stripes and decals, but does pick up the neat flexible rubber rear spoiler fitted to the RS1800/2000. Wheels are 5.5in. wide white-painted pressed steel.

European-bred car with good old Oz toughness and reliability.

There's no doubt the revised interior layout is attractive and pleasnat. The seats (apart from the clammy vinyl upholstery) are very comfortable and in all but the L version they are adjustable for rake. Back seat room is a little limited, but after all it is a small car. Front seat travel is quite generous, however at its limit it practically amputates rear seat passenger's legs.

The improved visibility is immediately noticeably and the revised instrument panel is both appealing and functional. We think three column stalks is going a bit far, but generally the ergonomic layout is acceptable.

Only the Ghia gets a glovebox, but L and XL versions have lots of under-dash shelf space for goodies.

The driving position is good for most, even tall drivers, but the steering column offset can be a bit strange at first. Interior trim fit has been excellent on all the Escorts we've seen and the quality of the finish as a whole is a tribute to the efficiency of the production workers at Ford's Homebush (Sydney) assembly plant.

DRIVING REPORT

CHANGES in construction wrought by the new skins which have been grafted onto the old underbody have resulted in a stiffer body and reduced scuttle shake. Weight has been increased slightly, but the car is pretty well balanced and is obviously the end product of some pretty thorough redesigning.

PERFORMANCE
AGAINST the clock our Escort Escapee test car was not as impressive as some of its competitors in a straight line, covering 0-100 km/h in 16.7 seconds and the Standing 400m in 20.7 seconds. By comparison the Gemini covers the same ground in 12.7 secs and 18.9 secs respectively. Admittedly the Gemini figures were recorded on a pre-ADR27a model, but the General has suffered less under the emissions regulations and there is very little difference in performance for the current Gemini.

In overtaking tests however the Escort proved to be not far away from its main competitor. Gemini's torque is greater (according to factory supplied figures), but it peaks at 4000 rpm, whereas Escort's torque peaks at only 2500 rpm.

MODERN MOTOR, FEBRUARY 1977

This gives the little Ford quite reasonable times in the gears. From 60-100 km/h in fourth the Escort is only eight tenths of a second slower than Gemini, but at 50-80 km/h it is almost a second faster, and between 80-110 km/h it is seven tenths faster.

It was our general consensus the Escort felt to be going a lot quicker than it actually was — I guess that says a lot for the red and yellow go-faster stripes. Despite significant differences in outright performance when Escort is compared to cars like Gemini and VW Golf the little Ford will give its owners satisfaction in most areas.

In all this talk about performance there remains the all-important economy factor. Under test (some 2500 km) our Escapee regularly returned 33mpg, and our best of 36.8mpg was returned three or four times, without too much concentration on economy driving techniques.

HANDLING
WHILE IT'S easy to measure performance data it's very difficult when it comes to summarising the handling aspects of various cars. The Escort proved a difficult car to make up our minds about.

Essentially it's a good handling car, but poor rear axle location does cause it to hop about unduly on broken surfaces. Initially the Escort is pretty neutral, breaking into slight oversteer when pressure is applied. However when really pushed to the limit I found the car became untidy in its response. I enjoyed pushing it hard on gravel rather than bitumen surfaces.

In an 8-car handling comparison test which Modern Motor conducted in the December '75 issue we rated Escort (in

BOOT is a useful size, with an upright-mounted spare to the left and the tiny fuel tank to the right.

overall handling) third, behind Gemini and Renault R12.

The small Ford is surefooted and light to handle, but a great deal of this must be attributed to the standard radial ply tyres. Our Escapee of course wore steel-belt radials on 5.5 rims and consequently it provided even better adhesion than standard cars.

We have absolutely no complaint with the braking system. The pressure required was quite high, but pedal 'feel' is progressive and there was no problems at all during the test program. Axle hop upset braking performance on corrugations, but the Escort generally was safe and stable under brakes.

We still get annoyed at the problem of 'force variation runout' which seems to have infected the Escort range, just like it has the Cortina series.

FVR is an industry term used to describe variations in tyre construction and its effect as the wheel revolves. It feels like the wheels are out of balance, but after a wheel balance the problem remains.

Ford product engineers know about the problem, but the Company seems content to live with it. The problem reflects both the quality of locally-supplied tyres and engineering efforts aimed at ironing it out, but I'll tell you something, we haven't struck the problem to any degree in GM-H cars.

SUMMARY
THE NEW Escort is an honest car. With its high equipment levels it matches the Japanese cars adequately and not only that it's more sporting to drive, handles better and of course has the back up of the Ford Motor Company and its dealer network.

Quality control is going to be the key to Escort's future, so we hope it remains at its current high. The facelift has gone very deep and produced a better car than its predecessor, which only makes your choice of car in this market segment even harder. ∎

ENGINE BAY is a maze of cables, tubes and anti-pollution equipment, but access is reasonable. Heavy bonnet will give women drivers stronger arm muscles.

The mean Escort

THERE would be no denying the fact that small imported cars like the Volkswagen Golf and the Mazda 323 have had a heavy impact on the local light-car market.

Both General Motors-Holden and Ford have felt the pinch — a situation that has led to appeals to the Federal Government for a reduction in sales tax and threatened mass retrenchments that could leave the market and the vehicle manufacturers reeling.

The circumstances are complex, and it is not easy to point out all the factors that have been acting together to bring about the depressed market situation.

However, one major factor has been public reaction to locally produced vehicles when they are directly compared to imported units.

If a potential buyer is presented with a choice between a conventional local product and a better, though more expensive, imported product, he will often switch to the higher priced unit.

The obvious solution is to improve the local product and regain at least part of the lost market share.

Pssst . . . wanna know where all those old Cortina engines went? Try lifting the lid on the new Ford Escort . . .

This is what has happened with quick re-thinks of models like the Torana and Cortina, resulting in more driveable cars — and more contented customers. The buyers are now swinging back to the local product, a fact illustrated by the market success of the Sunbird and the new Cortina.

The decision by Volkswagen Australia to cut its prices will put even more pressure on the locals because of the market coverage the range of Volkswagen and Audi cars have achieved in Australia.

It will now be up to General Motors-Holden, Ford and Chrysler to make sure they not only come up with the sort of products the public wants, but that they also maintain good quality control once those products are in production.

Ford's decision to upgrade its Escort with the 2-litre overhead-cam Cortina engine is a direct attempt to grab more of the light-car market.

With prices for the 2-litre Escort starting at $5100, the car will be competing strongly with Chrysler's Galant, General Motors-Holden's Gemini and Sunbird, Mazda's 808, Toyota's Corona and Datsun's 180B.

According to Ford, past sales of the Escort have been dominated by older buyers, so it would be a pretty safe bet that the flashy little Escort Escapee of 1976 was a deliberate attempt by Ford to see what sort of acceptance it could achieve if it openly appealed to the youth market. The strategy is by no means new — Ford has used it with great success in the past.

Now Ford has thrown in with the new 2-litre engine option a sports suspension package, rally pack, front spoiler and alloy wheels options — all good stuff for the youth market.

One important new option also available with the 2-litre engine will be factory air-conditioning.

MODERN MOTOR, SEPTEMBER 1977

Basically, the changes made to the Escort to allow it to take the bigger powerplant are:
● revised front end structure;
● forward shift of the radiator;
● new engine sump;
● bigger exhaust system;
● use of the bigger diameter Cortina clutch;
● revised rear axle ratio for better cruising and economy (from 3.77:1 to 3.54:1);
● beefier side gears in the differential to take increased engine torque;
● heavier steel tube walls in the front suspension struts;
● revised front spring and shock absorber rates.

A larger fuel tank — now 55 litres compared with 36 in the previous model — will give a greater cruising range and Ford has also increased the size of the boot by 16 percent. The fuel filler cap is now behind the rear number plate mount, and a dummy cover has been placed over the hole left in the imported rear quarter panels.

Seating has also been improved in the Escort with an across-the-board implementation of moulded seat pads, previously only available on Ghia models.

On the road, the 2-litre Escort has appreciably more power, but because the car was initially designed to be

The air cleaner dominates the engine bay, a sign of the anti-pollution regulations.

The driver's view of the 2.0-litre Escort fitted with the rally pack.

able to cope with the extra weight and power of a 2-litre engine, things don't get out of hand unless the Escort is pushed too hard. After all, the 2-litre unit is 30 percent up on power over the smaller 1600cc engine.

When we took the car out to Sydney's Amaroo Park for an evaluation drive and photographic session, it proved to be a very spirited little performer, with plenty of mid-range torque and heaps of controllable power, both on dirt and black-top surfaces.

Again, it's going to be a question of whether Ford can maintain quality-control on the Escort production line. There's no real reason why it shouldn't and if it does, it's going to have one hell of a hard goer on its hands.

With present market indicators what they are, the 2-litre Escort will be a most appealing unit to young buyers, whereas the snappier Ghia version — especially the air-conditioned version — will appeal more to the up-market and older buyer.

The entire Escort range now covers nine different models: the 1.6L 2-door sedan and van priced at $4492 and $4317; the 1.6GL 2-door, 1.6GL 4-door and 1.6GL van priced at $4885, $5011 and $4709 respectively; the 2.0GL 2-door, 2.0GL 4-door and 2.0GL van priced at $5100, $5226 and $4880; and the 2-litre Ghia 4-door at $5828. □

MODERN MOTOR, SEPTEMBER 1977

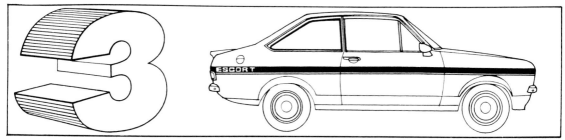

The Escort gets guts

Ford has transformed the traditionally
sluggish Escort into a zappy little performance
car by equipping it with — amongst other
things — a 2-litre engine

"BUT, GRANDMA, what big teeth you have."

"All the better to gobble up the kilometres, my dear."

"And what are all those stripes and spoilers and air dams you're wearing?"

"All the better to get across my new image, my dear."

Quicker than you, or even Roger Clarke, could wander through the woods, Ford has transformed old Grandma Escort into a wolfy little performance machine.

From being the small-car slug it was yesterday, suddenly the Escort now offers about the highest performance-for-the-dollar ratio of any car on the Australian market.

Till now, that rally-bred image of the Escort was something Australians could only read about. With the exception of a handful of early twin-cams and a limited run of RS2000s, we had to content ourselves with 1300cc Escorts perched on bicycle wheels.

But that has all changed with the option of the 2-litre engine. At the same time as giving the Escort proper power, Ford has slotted options and new standard equipment which make it a proper car.

Even enthusiasts will find appeal in the Escort. And that is obviously part of Ford's plan.

In England, the backbone of club motorsport is the Escort, which is available there in a variety of performance versions. Till now, only Japanese cars made much sense here for motorsport amateurs.

It would please Ford greatly if that changed, and there is no reason why it won't.

Not that car club-type people buy lots of cars. Rather, they are recognised as opinion leaders: a lot of buyers question people who are obviously interested in cars about an intending purchase. And that means enthusiasts can influence a very wide section of the market.

Perhaps it is significant that the other weekend we noticed no fewer than three 2-litre Escorts at a car-club motorkhana.

Not that the 2-litre Escort is an instant racer. In its present form, the overhead cam engine develops 70 kW, about 9 kW down on the figure quoted when the RS2000 was first released.

And Ford has chosen to cut back acceleration in favour of better economy at high-cruising speeds by using a relatively high ratio 3.54 to 1 rear axle. This gearing lets the engine loaf along, with 2000 rpm corresponding to a road speed of 60 km/h. But that is still a good enough

MODERN MOTOR, DECEMBER 1977

The back-to-front Escort label is appropriately on the spoiler; it spoils the car's front-on appearance.

power-to-weight ratio to give the car very respectable performance.

The 2-litre engine is flexible enough to let it pull fairly low in top, but naturally the particularly high final drive does mean that a lot of traffic work is done in third gear.

When you use the gearbox to advantage, you do find the overall higher ratios mean that, for a given situation, you are often in a cog lower than you might be in the more conventional buzz-box.

The third is great through moderately fast twisty stuff and for overtaking at highway speeds.

Our rally-packed test car came with a tacho, which — rather interestingly — wears no red-line. However, power drops off fairly rapidly around 6000 rpm so there is no point in exceeding that limit, which is really quite enough for a cooking 2-litre engine.

Competition versions certainly rev higher, but there is a lot to be done under the skin to make that a safe practice.

The gearbox itself is the same old Escort unit, with a change so light you can practically throw the lever from one slot to the next. However, the lever has a poor relationship to the seat and third gear is an uncomfortable reach for most drivers. Ford would do well to make the stick longer and bend it back towards the driver.

Now that it has the power to appeal to people who want performance, the Escort is available with options which give it a "competition" appearance.

These include a glass-fibre air-dam below the front bumper, a spoiler on the boot lid and 5.5in-wide alloy wheels.

Our test car was tricked up in this way and was also fitted with the optional sports suspension pack which comprises a stiffer front anti-roll bar, a rear anti-roll bar and stiffer springs and shock absorbers.

We half-expected the extra weight of the bigger engine up front to spoil the previous "driveability" of the Escort.

There is a difference

JUST HOW far removed is the 2-litre Escort from its rally-winning cousins?

Well, that depends on how serious you are about winning rallies. If you are content to have a careful run in club events and are prepared to slow up over the really rough bits, some reasonably mild modifications should keep it in one piece.

The engine, transmission and diff could be left standard. A substantial sump guard, mounted to the frame and not the cross member, would be a must. Now the tank is slung low under the boot, you would need a guard for that, too. Better, it should be relocated.

To use a near-standard car like that, you would have to drive very much within limits. But there is just about no end to what you can, and really must, do if you are serious about rallying an Escort.

The RS2000 Escort is basically the same as the Australian 2-litre, so the modifications staffer Jim Sullivan has made to his NBN TV/Kloster Ford RS2000 give some idea of what is necessary.

The car has an engine built for reliability and turning out around 105 kW on dual downdraught Webers. The engine uses special con-rods, pistons, valves and a toughened crank for obvious reasons.

The suspension uses special Bilstein struts, stronger coil springs, different rear springs and Bilstein rear shock absorbers. The strut towers have strengthened mounting points.

The major component change is the rear axle, which is a "mini-atlas" unit that is a lot more robust, and is fitted with a special strengthening plate.

It uses a limited-slip differential with a 4.6 to 1 ratio.

Larger rear brake drums from a Capri V6 are used, while ventilated discs replace the normal solid discs at the front.

A special front stabiliser bar mounting kit is used, which has much more substantial mountings.

A full alloy roll cage is mounted to a number of points inside the Escort.

However, the NBN TV/Kloster Ford car is only about a 50 percent job compared to the full-house version of Colin Bond. His beautifully-prepared car has the body extensively re-welded and plated. It also uses an entirely different front cross member.

And it still does not go as far as the full-house works rally cars . . .   □

MODERN MOTOR, DECEMBER 1977

The boot has been enlarged by relocating the fuel tank.

The heart of it all is the ex-Cortina 2-litre engine.

But, certainly in sports suspension form, it works better than ever. In fact, the handling is the type that sends you looking for corners.

The final limit of roadholding may not be in the ultimate bracket, but you can fling the Escort at corners and know it is going to go exactly where you plan it to go.

Occasionally, a bump will cause the cart springs at the rear to have a bit of a hiccup, but even then a flock of the wheel brings it back on line.

On dirt, it's magic and even the standard car does possess a lot of the marvellously predictable behaviour that is so evident in rally versions.

On tar, there is slight understeer with the power on, but the cornering line can be tightened merely by lifting the throttle. If you do hang the tail out, correction is a flick of the wrists. It's well balanced enough to be held on opposite lock on a wet road without any sign of drama.

It is easy and fun to drive. The sports suspension pack does make the ride a little harsher, but the benefits are more than worth this slight compromise.

Not so pleasing, on our particular test car, were the

brakes. When used hard, they vibrated badly and needed fairly high pedal pressures. They stopped the car satisfactorily, but they did not inspire confidence. In fairness, the test car had probably had a pretty harsh work-out.

To match the up-market move of the Escort, the interior has been revised slightly, but items like the door trim and the seats give away the vehicle's true age.

There is nothing particularly wrong with the function of the interior styling, but it is dated. There is no glovebox, but there is a centre console in addition to a parcel tray below the dashboard.

The instruments are grouped in front of the driver and, on our optioned-up test car, comprised a speedo with re-settable trip meter, tachometer, temperature gauge and fuel gauge.

Four-way hazard flashers and an electrically-heated rear window are standard.

A feature of the $360-odd rally pack (or Rallye Pack, as Ford calls it) is an intermittent windscreen wiper mode with a seven-second delay between wipes.

A continuing annoyance with the Escort is the use of a steering-column stalk as a light switch. There is no reason why this third stalk could not be merely a simple dashboard-mounted switch, avoiding the present situation where it is extremely easy to knock the switch to "on" when switching off the ignition. It is the right formula for a flat battery when the car is left parked for the day.

With its new-found performance, the Escort also deserves better seats. They are reasonably comfortable, but are too wide and shapeless, providing little lateral support. The rear seat is comfortable enough, but has precious little leg room.

Maybe in anticipation of enthusiastic driving, rally-style panic handles are mounted above each passenger position.

With power to carry a little more luggage, the latest Escort has a larger boot. This has been achieved by putting the fuel tank — which is also larger — beneath the floor, leaving clear the mudguard space formerly occupied by the tank.

The previous filler hole in the mudguard has been closed off with a simple blanking plate and it is great sport watching service station attendants try to "open" it.

The old Ford bogey of "finish is poor finish" is still evident in the Escort. The interior of the boot on the test car was particularly rough and a number of body rattles were evident.

On the other hand, general noise levels are particularly low. In part, this is due to a much less busy engine.

Particularly impressive was the fuel consumption of the Escort. The nature of the car invites fairly vigorous use and yet it still returned an overall test figure of 9.34 litres per 100 kilometres.

With a little more refinement, the 2-litre Escort would have to be a very good argument for not spending twice as much on a European exotic . . .   □

NEW RELEASES

Escort RS2000

Ford has put performance motoring back within the reach of everyone with the new Escort RS2000.

The RS2000 is a locally-made version of the droop-snoot Escort last seen here in 1976, when Ford imported 25 from Britain.

It's shaping up as one of the best-value cars of the year, combining affordable price with strong straight line performance, precise handling, and distinctive looks.

The bad news, though, is that stocks of the RS2000 are limited. The first shipment of 250, a large number of which were sold before they were delivered to dealers, will be followed by a production run of just 45 a month.

The Australian RS2000 is available in two body styles — two-door and four-door. The two-door costs around $6190 and the four-door about $6325, making them top-value fun cars if our memory of the imported RS2000 still holds.

Both versions went on sale on July 4, nearly two months later than planned. Prototypes were displayed at the Melbourne International Motor Show in March and were scheduled for release in May.

However, according to a senior Ford' executive, the delay was caused by a hold-up in ADR compliance for the special Scheel seats fitted as standard to the RS2000. Ford is the first manufacturer to offer specialist seats in a local model.

The RS2000 replaces the Rally Pack option in the Escort range. Standard powerplant is the two-litre engine with four-speed gearbox. Automatic transmission is optional. (Incidentally, all auto Escorts now have the same power and torque outputs as the manual versions — power is up by 7kW to 70kW, while torque has increased 8Nm to 148Nm.)

The only mechanical difference between the RS2000 and other two-litre Escorts is the short-throw gear-shift pattern.

Exterior add-ons included in the RS2000 package are sloping RIM plastic front, quad 14.5cm quartz halogen headlights, black paint-outs, rear spoiler, and styled steel wheels (alloy Volantes are optional). Five colour choices are available: red, yellow, orange, dark metallic blue, and white — all with black interiors.

The sports handling option is standard, which means you get uprated spring and shock absorber rates, and a rear stabiliser bar.

Inside, sports steering wheel and instrumentation, twin Scheel seats, and matching cloth trim on the rear seats complete the performance package. Air conditioning is available as an option.

MODERN MOTOR, August 1979

A fast (but noisy) fun car

THERE IS ONE word that sums up everything about Ford's Escort RS2000 — fun.

The RS2000 is a fun car to drive, a fun car to own, a fun car to have fun in.

And, strangely enough, most of its appeal comes from the image it has. Because when you strip away the plastic nose, bright paint, and tape stripes, the RS2000 is really nothing more than the previous Rally Pack 2.0-litre Escort.

The shovel-nosed model will do a lot to enhance the overall image of the Escort range. It adds some life to an otherwise dull line-up of models.

The RS2000 is probably the closest you'll get to driving a rally car on the road. Its forest racer heritage, the kickback of years of Escort participation in rallying worldwide, is apparent in its sharpness on the road.

It's also a bargain car. The test car, a four-door, retails at just $6513, plus $224 for the optional alloy wheels and $103 for the laminated windscreen — a total of $6840 for one of the most enjoyable cars we've driven for a long time.

The low cost of the RS2000 models — there's a two-door as well — means almost everyone can have a sporty performance car. And when we say performance, we mean performance.

The Australian RS2000, which is different in many ways to the English version, is one of the fastest cars on the road. Its light weight and powerful 2.0-litre, four-cylinder engine give it rapid acceleration.

Out on the highway, where the RS2000 really feels good, it just sings along at between 140 and 160 km/h and gets close to 170 km/h for its top speed. So you can imagine that at the legal 100/110 km/h highway limits around the country it's only loafing along.

The only thing that we didn't like was the noise. It's a very noisy little car. Around town you don't mind that because the growly exhaust is part of its charm. But at high speed, the din — both mechanical and road induced, is very high.

Also, the RS2000 is particularly susceptible to sidewinds, and tends to wander more than you'd expect in blustery conditions.

Otherwise, the Escort RS2000's stability is excellent. Its pin-sharp rack-and-pinion steering is tremendously accu-

rate. Few cars have as much feel and responsiveness through the steering, which is enhanced by the special sports steering wheel that's part of the package.

The RS2000 sits very flat on the road. The uprated shock absorbers and anti-roll bars combine with firmer springing to produce a particularly solid and steady cornering stance.

The ride is very comfortable. There is very little harshness transmitted through to the passenger compartment, and suspension travel is sufficient to stop bottoming on rough roads or over humps.

Handling is generally close to neutral until you start driving enthusiastically through tight corners.

Over our high speed interstate run we averaged 12.1 litres per 100km, which shows the RS2000 combines performance with fuel economy. The best figure we saw during the test was 10 litres for every 100km.

The only drawback of the all-cloth interior trim is that it's available in one color only — black — which gets very hot in warm weather. Also, even in the four-door version, rear space is very cramped — a sign of the age of the Escort design.

Apart from the sports instruments and radio, the RS2000 dash is very bare. In front of the passenger there's just an expanse of black plastic.

The Escort RS2000 is a way of putting fun back into driving. It's the kind of car we should all be driving — responsive, accurate, economical, and fast.

– Mark Fogarty

Ford Escort RS 2000

ENGINE

Cylinders	Four
Bore x Stroke	90.8 x 76.9 mm
Capacity	1998 cc
Carburation	Twin-throat down-draught
Compression Ratio	9.2 to 1
Claimed Power	70 kW at 5200 rpm
Claimed Torque	148 Nm at 3800 rpm

TRANSMISSION

Type	Four-speed manual
Gearbox Ratios	
First	3.65
Second	1.97
Third	1.37
Fourth	1.00
Final Drive Ratio	3.54

SUSPENSION

Front	Independent by MacPherson struts; integral anti-roll bar/tension rod.
Rear	Leaf springs; anti-roll bar.
Wheels	5.0 JJ x 13
Tyres	ZR 70S x 13
Steering	Rack-and-pinion

BRAKES

Front	244 mm discs
Rear	223 mm drums

DIMENSIONS AND WEIGHT

Wheelbase	2405 mm
Front Track	1270 mm
Rear Track	1296 mm
Overall Length	4109 mm
Overall Width	1596 mm
Overall Height	1373 mm
Ground Clearance	146 mm
Kerb Weight	1000 kg
Fuel Tank Capacity	54.6 litres

CALCULATED DATA

Weight to Power	14.29 kg/kW
Specific Power Output	35.04 kW/litre

PERFORMANCE

Fuel Consumption	12.1 litres/100km
Standing 400 Metres	17.9 seconds
0-100 km/h	11.5 seconds
Top Speed	168 km/h
Braking from 100 km/h	46.6 metres

MODERN MOTOR, November 1979